MY FAMILY
AND ME

Fifty Years of General Practice

1960s and onwards

By

Dr Jane Little

ISBN-13: 978-1544883939
ISBN-10: 1544883935

To my ever-patient husband who has supported me throughout my years in practice and during the writing of these memoirs.

CONTENTS

While all the stories in this book are true, some names and identifying details have been changed to protect the privacy of the people involved.

1. The Beginning

On my first day in General Practice I knew I had made the biggest and worst mistake of my life. My last hospital job had been in a frenetically busy, modern obstetric unit working with a team of doctors. I had loved every minute of it, but now, here I was, about to start on the branch of medicine I had always dreamt about. To have continuity of care, really get to know patients and look after the whole person.

The silence was oppressive.

I turned my newly acquired key in the front door quarter of an hour before the morning surgery was due to begin. Glancing at the baize notice board in the outside porch I noted several prescriptions waiting to be collected. I had observed, when accompanying my new partners-to-be on an introductory week, there had had queues outside waiting for consultations to start.

This was silence on a big scale. Dressed in my new smart outfit I had expected to be welcomed and to begin work immediately. It was a dismal September day. There was no one at all in the waiting room. Eventually an elderly gentleman arrived and I almost ran to greet him. But, no, he would wait to see the 'proper' doctor. The next, a much younger gentleman, announced he would get the bus up the hill to the doctor he was used to seeing. The only person I treated that entire morning was a small child screaming with earache.

In the early 1960s it was all much like the good old days of Drs Finlay and Cameron. But, of course, the NHS had come into being, with consultations and medicines free to all. Doctors knew their patients and patients knew who their doctors were. Patients also had their very own doctor who would almost certainly be available day or night whenever illness struck. Failing their very own doctor, then it would be another from the same small practice. The patient trusted the doctor's decisions and carried them out almost invariably without question.

My consulting rooms were initially rented from my two partners. The consulting room itself was the middle room of the ground floor in a three-storey terraced house. There was my comfortable 'deacon's' chair, a large desk with drawers down each side, a couple of plain patients' chairs, a sink with steriliser, instruments and glass syringes on the draining board, a book case and a metal filing cabinet. The wallpaper might have been patterned at one time, and so might the carpet. The only light came from a small pair of grubby French windows facing north. I had imported a couple of standard lamps to augment the dismal central light. The front room was the waiting room that doubled as the caretaker's dining room on Sundays. The tattered magazines were then removed from the table to be replaced on the Monday morning. The decor and temperature were equally dismal. (On one memorable freezing cold January day, a white-coated man walked purposefully in, disconnected the electric fire, and marched out with it!)

The room at the rear was the caretaker's kitchen to which she had no access during surgery hours. Then only private practices had receptionists and only my senior partners had very part-time secretaries. My trusty pen was busy.

Until recently, after fifty years in practice, I still worked half a day a week. The contrast in premises is unimaginable. This was a multi-roomed, modern, well-equipped surgery with computers, receptionists, nurses, secretaries, counsellors, chiropodists and many, many others. Everything is clinically spotless with sterile areas.

Today record keeping is almost entirely on the computer and as accurate as possible, with every detail noted – partly for legal purposes (so essential nowadays), but mainly because more than one doctor will be seeing the patient. The choice of medicines is now so vast that the numerous side effects or possible interactions need to be spotted quickly. Thankfully computer programs highlight possible problem areas.

Then, records were perfunctory and in many cases not at all. The familiar 'Lloyd George' envelope to hold the records is, unbelievably the same then as now – except today it bulges over, the contents usually being transferred to a thick A4 folder. (Paper records kept for legal purposes – why??) In the very near future everything will be totally paperless. In the 1960s only a few letters from hospitals actually reached the files and only rarely was information written in the notes.

My then senior partner assured me he learnt to carry all the essentials about his own patients in his head. This was just possible then, but it was not good – he died very unexpectedly after a minor operation leaving all the information still inside his head. We each had a half-day off each week and two short weekends in three. This included the nights. There were Saturday morning surgeries, of course. The weekend duty doctor also did one on Saturday evenings. Many patients now keep referring to the good old days, but the workload then was hugely different from now. The hours were theoretically very much longer. Prescribing was limited. The British National Formulary ('BNF' issued by the NHS to each doctor – now also online) was a thin booklet – it is now a massive, thick, unwieldy tome. Today's GP expects to work about forty hours a week in theory, but in practice it takes twice as long – eighty hours is much nearer the norm. There are always extras, emergencies, a mass of forms, complicated claim applications and administrative duties. Add at least one meeting a week, probably more. Then there is personal audit, audit of other doctors, hospital visits – and you can begin to understand what all the fuss is about now. Far too much of the doctor's time is given to duties other than seeing patients. Locum doctors have the pleasure of doing exactly what they were trained to do – seeing patients full-time.

Weekend and night emergencies are now covered by various agencies, some good, some bad, but rarely in the way the patient would wish to be seen. We might have been disturbed by one or two visits during night hours, plus a couple of phone calls. My GP daughter says the agency will now receive up to sixty calls during the night covering the same number of patients two ordinary sized practices would look after.

Women doctors were relatively rare in 1960. There was considerable prejudice against us, but in a contrary way they were also much in demand. Some patients felt intimidated by the (then – not now) very smartly dressed 'superior' male doctors who were well off and played golf, and felt a woman doctor would be more empathetic.

For the first few weeks I despaired of any patient ever signing on with me. It was a very slow start. This branch surgery was in a very old-fashioned, deprived area. The rail, construction and manual workers were not at all keen to be seen a woman doctor. However, it was men from the 'gay' community who were among my first patients. Homosexuality was illegal at the time. Male doctors disliked having them on their lists. Many of them were musicians or actors and they were all delightful, gentle and thoughtful people. Many a theatre or opera ticket came my way to be greatly enjoyed by my husband and myself. Living within easy reach of the London entertainment world we had a goodly number of them to look after. Now, there are almost more women GPs than men and there is no discrimination against homosexuality – at least in theory.

Some of my patients were memorable for one reason or another. These are the ones of whom I have written. The names are fictitious, but their stories are authentic. My practice was in a London suburb that I trust cannot be identified. It was a densely populated area with a succession of immigrants from Jamaica, Hungary, Poland, Hong Kong, Uganda, India, Pakistan, Bangladesh and Vietnam among others.

By the time I retired as senior partner there were more immigrants on my list than indigenous people. I had six full-time partners including some from Asia, and two part-time ladies. It was as up to date as was possible for a very modern surgery to be – clean, fresh containing every equipment needed to enable us to carry out as many procedures as possible. We had one partner who specialised in minor surgery, another in treating arthritis, one particularly interested in diabetes and so on. My principal interests were gynaecology and obstetrics.

2. What If…

It was late. An hour after Evening Surgery should have finished. It was not my 'on call' night. I was looking forward to a quiet meal with my other half and tucking into a good book for what was left of the evening. It had been truly hectic. A number of extras had been slotted in and, for once, they were all genuinely in need of immediate attention. The duty receptionist (yes, we did have a couple by 1972) was as tired as I was. Just as I had placed my stethoscope in the drawer and was locking the prescription pad away she tapped on the door and came in rather tentatively. I looked up expecting her to ask if I would lock up and she could get off home. Instead, she ventured a little hesitantly, "Mr and Mrs Finch have just come in, and, well, it sounds serious." I looked at my watch and about to say a very firm 'no'. "Please," she pleaded, "I know Angela really well and they are the most uncomplaining people you could possibly meet. She looks terrible." Reluctantly, and if I'm honest, inwardly fuming, I agreed, told her to ring my home and then to go home herself.

I pulled out a second chair and invited them to sit down. They had been patients of the practice for many years, but I could not recall having met either of them before. He was well over six feet tall, very thin, and looked exhausted. She was a forty-five year old well-built woman with a head of beautiful chestnut hair down to her shoulders. She did indeed look ill.

He opened the consultation. "We've just driven back from our holiday in Lyme Regis and come straight here."

I must have inadvertently shown my irritation. Angela interrupted. "Oh, I told him we shouldn't bother you, but this headache is so severe and he gets so worried about me. We saw the doctor down there twice and he's given me these pills and says it's a sort of migraine. Really, I know it will go, only, only it's been there for three days now and it's getting worse and worse. And my vision is funny." Her fingers were firmly placed just behind her left ear.

Many doctors claim to have sixth sense alerting them to something significant. Not easy to explain how they reached the diagnosis. It is, of course, that computer we call 'brain' sometimes processing information more quickly than we can follow. I didn't say anything or even examine her but picked up the phone and rang the admissions doctor at our major hospital, meanwhile asking them to wait outside. Eventually he answered and with a great deal of persuasion agreed to contact the regional neurosurgical unit. Without waiting for an answer, I scribbled a few lines on a piece of notepaper (protocol demands every admission is accompanied by a letter or, nowadays, fax or e-mail) and rang for an emergency ambulance to take her to the unit. Even this took time. Neurosurgical units normally only take from other hospitals, not directly from GPs, but the urgency was impressed upon them. I really didn't care how she got to the neurosurgical unit as long as she got there. Very apprehensively, in case I had overreacted and my diagnosis was wrong, I too left the surgery, locked up and went home to the remains of a meal.

Later, unable to sleep I went quietly downstairs and rang the hospital. Angela was still in the operating theatre. There was no information available, but if I liked they would ring me when it was all over. I did like, and crawled back to bed. It seemed probable my diagnosis was right. I hoped we had been in time to save her life. It was nearly seven in the morning before the phone call came. She was out of the theatre, deeply unconscious and on the critical list. It had indeed been a sub-arachnoid haemorrhage. Round the base of the brain is a circle of blood vessel with the all-important brain supply of blood vessels leading from it. Sometimes, fortunately rarely, people are born with little weaknesses in this circle and at some stage in life the weakness can give way with blood escaping into the brain. This leads to an intense headache and, if a big one, may result in instant death. In this case it was a tiny leak that hadn't sealed by itself. As the pool of blood increased, so did the headache, eventually putting pressure on the part of the brain responsible for vision.

I saw a lot of Angela after her discharge from hospital some weeks later. She had survived, but at a price. She was partially sighted, indeed almost blind, and needed a great deal of care. However, she did gradually improve over the next couple of years and enjoyed a reasonable quality of life. Never once did I hear her express any anger towards the doctor at Lyme Regis. Her husband came to see me once to talk about it, but refused to put in any complaint. Headaches, as he said, are common. Very common. In medicine we always say "common things are commonest". She had

had migraine in the past. He had been perfectly happy with the diagnosis until the journey home, when he decided a second opinion would be helpful.

It was one of those situations that assume nightmare proportions at two o'clock in the morning making one cringe to think what would have happened if… really, *if* my receptionist had not put in a quiet word, *if* Angela had not had years of never visiting the doctor, and *if* my sixth sense had not overcome my tiredness. Had I refused to see her I am perfectly certain they would have gone home, nice people as they were, and planned to wait until the next morning – by which time she would have been dead.

3. Appearances Are Not What They Seem

Maddy was forty-five years old and unmarried. She was an only child of older parents, very protected and rigidly brought up in a deeply religious household. When she left school with skills in shorthand and typing she joined the typing pool of a huge insurance company. This was the 1970s. By the time I saw her she had risen to become a supervisor. Her father had died some years previously. Mother was a demanding, whinging semi-invalid who delighted in occupying all of Maddy's spare moments. I found the mandatory monthly visit to mother in their home a chore. The modern second-storey flat was dull and spotless. The inevitable three china mallards flew over the tiled mantelpiece. She always had a long list of what Maddy did not manage to do. The mantle-shelf needed a proper clean. The windows were grimy. The flowers needed fresh water. Her head was bad and Maddy had forgotten to get her tablets. Her back hurt. And so on. There was no real reason why she should not see to most things herself. Poor Maddy had never had the opportunity to make a life for herself, let alone find a partner and marry. Her major outing was to her church on Sundays.

On the occasion I first saw her she had been a patient on my list for a number of years, but apart from trivia had never previously needed attention. The initial diagnosis was easy. She had 'yellow jaundice'. My job was to find out what sort of jaundice she had and the reason it had developed. It would take a whole book to give all the causes of jaundice, but basically, either something is obstructing the outflow of bile from the gall bladder (sending the yellow pigment backwards into the blood stream), or something is damaging blood cells and releasing yellow pigment. The latter is often a virus – infective hepatitis – and the former can be a gallstone, or cirrhosis of the liver just to give a couple of examples. A series of blood tests can give a diagnosis. Meanwhile, after a careful examination I arranged this and gave her a medical certificate to be off work for the next two weeks. From the clinical point of view this appeared to be a viral infection. She was unwell, but not too bad. I did feel sorry for her trying to rest at home with mother making all her usual demands.

Two weeks later she reappeared to renew her medical certificate, flopped into the chair looking considerably more ill. The blood tests had confirmed it to be, in all probability, a viral infection. Her liver felt more enlarged than before but this disease can take time before resolving – which it almost always does. I arranged further blood tests and asked her to come back in a week. This time when palpating her abdomen as well as the enlarged liver I had felt a lump low down. I was sure it had not been there before. I began to wonder if she perhaps had a tumour complicating the picture or perhaps a large fibroid. Many middle-aged women get muscle lumps in the wall of the womb. It was in the days before scans or many of the diagnostic facilities we take for granted today. A fibroid is a lump of muscle-like tissue with enough density to show up in an x-ray. At least an x-ray might be helpful, I thought, before sending her to hospital for further investigations for her jaundice. A couple of hours later the radiographer rang from the local cottage hospital. She was hysterical with laughter and could barely get the words out. The staff was dining out on it. Yes, of course you have guessed it. But you never met Maddy, or you wouldn't have believed it either. Lovely as she was, she was most unfortunate in her looks, very mannish and ungainly. It was pregnancy. All four and a half months of it. What on earth was I to do? I had a whole week in which to think. Abortions at this time were very, very difficult to get, but it had to be offered.

Her appointment time came – I had asked for a double slot. Her jaundice looked slightly better, but not much. I told her the result of the x-ray. She looked at me totally bemused and told me not to be utterly ridiculous. It was impossible. She had never had any relationship with any man and believed in only one virgin birth. They had got her x-ray mixed up with someone else's. I, too, had felt this so strongly I had actually gone to view it. I gave up, knowing time, if nothing else, would prove it to be only too correct. Meanwhile I handed over another certificate. I really did not know how to handle the situation.

A couple of weeks later a call came from the insurance company's medical officer. Just, he said, to ask how much longer Maddy's jaundice was likely to last and would I like to refer her privately, at their expense, to a specialist? I cannot remember what I muttered but it obviously had not sounded convincing.

He persisted. "Were there, um, any other problems with Maddy?" I must have hesitated for too long. "Could there be any difficulty in telling me what the problem is?" he asked.

"Yes," I admitted, "there is another problem but as yet I'm not at liberty to disclose it."

"Well," he continued, "may I venture to suggest either she is having a nervous breakdown or she is pregnant?"

I was stunned. "Why do you ask?"

"Because," he answered, "the warehouse man is in court tomorrow for raping a member of staff and attempted rape of another. A couple of the typing pool asked to see me this morning. Maddy had been absent from work for a long time now, which had made them think they needed to go to someone in authority. They had seen Maddy in a hysterical and dishevelled state in the staff toilet about four or five months ago, frantically trying to get her clothes on properly. They had just found out about the other girls. They remembered Maddy had been having problems with getting a new typewriter delivered from the warehouse. As she had been away from work for so long they wondered if the episode had anything to do with her illness."

I was able to say the jaundice was genuine enough but, yes, she was indeed pregnant and far too advanced to consider an abortion.

Next time there was no alternative other than to confront her with the story the medical officer had related. Silently she twisted her hands in her lap as the tears poured down her face into her lap. "I thought," she whispered, "it was being a middle-aged spinster made me have such terrible thoughts. I couldn't tell even you about the nightmares because I thought you would just tell me it was because I was so repressed, and it was normal. I wake up every night two or three times dreaming that is what happened and try not to cry out and wake Mum. You read these things in magazines but I never believed they happened in real life."

At least we could now make rational plans. We had several weeks before Mother would think anything other than Maddy was putting on weight. After a great deal of persuasion Mother agreed Maddy should go to Brighton to recuperate from her long illness. She knew the insurance company had a base there and agreed the sea air would indeed help her to recover fully. The pastor of their church, who I knew well, was even more than helpful. He arranged a care home for Mother and a mother and baby home for Maddy, both of which were associated with their church.

The baby was duly born. Maddy had made the most of her time in the home – she was at least twice the age of the other residents, but having a great deal of common sense was able to offer help to many of them. The baby was adopted. Each year, on his birthday, until he was sixteen she received a photograph of him. She shared them with me. He looked a very happy boy indeed. Best of all, her mother loved the care home so much she opted to stay there permanently, enabling Maddy to branch out to sing in her church choir and join in their other activities. Her employer, the insurance company, was very tactful. She was transferred to a small branch nearer home. The young man involved got a very long prison sentence.

4. *Every Doctor Has One*

Every doctor has the occasional 'heart-sink' patient – the one seen on the appointment list who gives rise to the inward groan and the voiced "not him (or her) again!" My first senior partner was a very kind and loveable Irishman. He had several such patients. He assured me I too would have many such during my time in practice. Never, he said, never ignore their complaints. On a less busy day do a thorough examination from top to toe. You might find you like the patient a bit better afterwards, and you will not have the worry of missing something important. Remember even 'heart-sink' patients get serious diseases and die. I learnt this to my cost some years later. I had a demanding German lady who was at least a three times weekly attender at the surgery. Basically she was lonely, her English appalling and her salesman husband never seemed to be around. One day I remembered the good advice I had been given and tried to examine her. She refused to remove her clothes despite having come to seek help for her cough – yet again. Rather roughly, I fear, I forced her vest lower to listen and saw to my utter horror a huge fungating cancer of the breast.

Joanne was a 'heart-sink' patient from my very first week in practice until the day I retired from that practice thirty-five years later. She still writes every Christmas and even came to visit me in my retirement several counties away. The only child of very elderly parents, she was overindulged, emotionally very childish and not very bright. She had survived normal schooling with a great deal of absence and not much joy. Her problem throughout the time I was in practice centred round her weight – which was considerable. She was not quite five feet in height and her weight rarely dipped below twelve stone. On occasions it was considerably more. Back in the 1960s amphetamines were commonly prescribed to dampen the appetite in those attempting to slim. She had them. They had no effect on her weight, but she did become addicted to them. It was a nightmare getting her to stop taking them. She would cry and scream, lie on the floor and kick her heels into the air like a baby. My only course was to leave the room until the hysterics had passed. Then we would try to reach a rational way of treatment where neither of us would lose face. I would cut down the dose and offer one of the newer supposedly non-addictive drugs that were beginning to come onto the market.

She was exceptionally demanding and manipulative. On one awful occasion, technically, I should have been struck off the medical register! To this day I remain surprised there was no sequel. It was evening surgery in the days when patients came and waited their turn. Appointment systems had yet to come. Neither had we the luxury of an evening receptionist. I had seen Joanne in the waiting room which gave me the usual sinking feeling. An urgent call came in from the midwife who needed me immediately. I put my head round the waiting room door, surveyed the ring of patients, apologised, said I would be back, but if their problem was not urgent would suggest they should come back tomorrow. Joanne started shouting saying she had to see me then and couldn't possibly wait. Ignoring her, I collected my bags and went out to the car. Unlocked as usual. There was Joanne sitting in the passenger seat, crying hysterically. Having very forcibly told her to get out, I walked round to the passenger side and tried to pull her out – unsuccessfully. I got back into the driving seat, swivelled round and with both feet kicked her out into the rose bed. I leant across, closed the door and drove off. It was a genuine emergency and very late before I opened my own front door – only to be greeted by my husband informing me there was a very scratched and upset young lady in our sitting room…

Huddled in an armchair with a rug round her shoulders, an un-drunk cup of tea beside her and sobbing hysterically, was Joanne. She had walked well over one and a half miles to reach my home. She lived all of a mile and a half in the opposite direction. My immediate reaction was she could jolly well walk home! Too tired to argue, I ordered her into the car without a single glance at her scratches. We had a silent drive there. I would like to say she never abused knowing my home address again, but I cannot.

There were times when she became sufficiently depressed to be admitted to hospital – almost invariably being discharged within a few days labelled, quite correctly, 'personality disorder'. When she was about thirty-five years of age she met John, another patient of the same age. He was as thin as she was fat but far more sensible. Yes, I did attend the wedding. And yes, she did continue her frequent visits, but they were much less demanding. Her parents set them up in their own home where she managed surprisingly well. John was a keen photographer and Joanne became interested too. Oddly enough I was actually rather fond of her!

5. Not Home from Home

Mrs Reuben was another heart-sink patient, but instinctively I felt sorry for her without quite knowing why. She was a large, blousy, middle-aged Jewish lady with auburn dyed hair, almost invariably wearing heavily tinted glasses. Her home was a five-bedroom detached house in a salubrious area. Most of my practice was in a crowded working-class area, but once a week I took a surgery in my senior partner's consulting room on his half-day off – hence Mrs Reuben. She always had multiple complaints including migraines, back pain, arthritic knees and stomach problems – among any other ones you can imagine. Patiently (though I say it of myself!), each week we would plough through her carefully written list of complaints. Unless the waiting room was very crowded I would examine one part of her and try my hardest to reassure her she would still be alive the following week.

It was several months before I got anywhere near the real problem. The dawning came not from her, but from a near neighbour who was particularly careful about her own position in society and the importance of keeping the neighbourhood exclusive. Really, the neighbour informed me, it was most terribly embarrassing to have a neighbour who not only drove a taxi (one of the black traditional London ones), but would go in and out of the drive at all hours of day and night and, and worst of all, left the taxi parked in the driveway for all to see! With a raised eyebrow I let this pass without comment. Possibly even surprised it wasn't followed up by an anti-Semitic remark as well – in which case I would have irreparably damaged the doctor-patient relationship.

Inevitably Mrs R. appeared the following Wednesday with the usual carefully written list. I listened, as usual, but asked as I had done many times before how her husband was faring. Fine, absolutely fine, no problems at all – he was never ill, but, oh, by the way he did need a medical for his job. She squirmed in her chair, looking very embarrassed. Rather than going through a long, evasive rigmarole and being fobbed off with some cover story, I replied immediately saying I knew taxi drivers had to pass a medical regularly, but he would need to make a special appointment as they took time. The relief was obvious and out came the whole miserable story.

These days we are all familiar, through the media, with unhappy lottery winners, though as yet I haven't met one happy or unhappy. She had lived in a two-up, two-down terraced house with a shared loo at the bottom of the yard in the east end of London. Slightly better off both in money and education than her neighbours, she had been a leading lady in the community enjoying endless noisy gossips along the road with her many friends and relatives. The East Street Market on Saturdays had been the highlight of her week. They did the football pools. I have no idea how much they won but it must have been considerable. The house alone was way beyond anything I could have ever contemplated buying. The son and daughter were both packed off to expensive boarding schools from which they returned openly despising their parents and counting the days when they could finally leave them behind. The husband at least tried to continue his only known occupation. This further alienated them from their neighbours. She had tried attending the local WI, but was not made welcome. They had tried visiting their previous neighbourhood with a view to returning there, but ended up feeling like strangers with no longer any connections to family or former friends. There was no occupation she could follow. Altogether she was one desperately lonely and sad lady whose one contact, other than with her husband, was her weekly jaunt to the surgery.

At least our consultations now had a rational basis, many of which were spent looking for a solution – even a partial one. Oddly enough it was her husband who was resistant to moving away from their luxury home. Eventually he saw his wife was becoming quite capable of taking her own life if he did nothing. They did sell up, and moved into a semi-detached house at some distance in a mixed-race area where there were other Jewish people. At this point I sadly lost contact with her. I genuinely liked her and missed her visits. She will never be happy again, but she might have found some reason to go on living. I just hope the children did not leave home altogether.

6. *Trainee or Registrar*

We became a Training Practice in the 1980s. In my day they were called 'Trainees' but now they have the title of 'Registrar' to align them with their hospital-based colleagues. They have already completed a five-year course at medical school, passed the final exams followed by at least two years in rotating hospital jobs. They came to us for a year, usually taking the exam for the Royal College of General Practitioners at the end. From our point of view we had to be subjected to scrutiny to ensure we were a suitable, totally up-to-date practice. One or more of us GPs had to attend a number of special training sessions to be taught how to train. I enjoyed it very much. We had over the years a procession of good, excellent and one or two indifferent trainees.

Only one had to be completely failed and he really was an oddity. Anthony was of some concern even in his induction fortnight before we dared let him loose to see patients on his own. He always came late — slightly in the mornings and very late for afternoon sessions. He had a strong Irish accent and was very 'laid back'. The proper normal pattern would be for him to complete a morning non-appointment surgery at his own pace, come in to me to review all he had done during that session and then do allocated and suitable home visits. A couple of afternoons he was expected to help with family planning, maternity or child health clinics and then to get on with an evening surgery which in those days began at 6 p.m. He should have attended one-to-one tutorials weekly. He would mysteriously disappear after morning surgery before his review time, and often not reappear before evening. Even getting angry with him and threatening to sack him brought little change. I threatened him with everything possible. The visits would get done after evening surgery. Not popular with patients. As he lived a good hour's travel from the surgery we were at a loss to know where he went during the day.

The answer came from Fred. Fred was my petrol pump attendant who looked after my car like a baby. He was a large, overweight, florid and happy alcoholic who had no wish to curtail the heavy drinking that seemed to stop just short of immediately killing him.

He was popular and well known to all in the neighbourhood. Especially in the pub next door. No, that was not where Anthony spent all his time. Fred was a rare visitor to the surgery but eventually he did have to come with a large untreated ulcerated leg. Unusual to see one quite so big, so I called Anthony in to have a look at it. Fred greeted him with great camaraderie much to Anthony's obvious embarrassment. Puzzled, I waited until Anthony had returned to his consulting room. Where, I asked Fred, had he met Dr X before? He roared with laughter. "In the betting shop! From mid-day to closing time he never leaves it!" In the evenings, after he had done one or two of his listed visits, he apparently met the same gang in the pub and drank rather heavily even by Fred's standards.

I called Anthony in immediately after Fred had left, telling him not to return again to our surgery – ever. He was reported to the authorities responsible for his training programme. They gave him a second chance at another practice that tolerated his behaviour much longer than we did. He never did qualify as a GP and I remain curious to know what did happen to him.

Probably the nicest and best trainee we had would have done well in today's society. However, he fell foul of the prejudices of the times, even though by this time homosexuality was no longer illegal. Paul was as near perfect as we could wish – highly intelligent, caring, resourceful, empathetic to patients and a joy to work with. Also extremely good looking with his black hair, blue eyes and immaculately tailored suits that showed off his fine figure. Time came to find him a practice at the end of his year with us. He had rather a public school accent so we found him, what we thought, was the ideal placement in a well-heeled neighbouring suburb. I had suspected he was 'gay' fairly early on. Oddly, even with hindsight, none of the others – doctors or staff – had suspected it. He moved in with his partner to a delightful house and all appeared to go from strength to strength. Living quietly with little, socialising, it all seemed ideal. Their way of life could upset nobody.

Then anonymous, unpleasant notes started to come through his door. They escalated, and letters began to arrive to the senior partner of the practice on a daily basis. Rumours started to spread. Gradually a number of patients refused to see him. Suggestive comments were made in front of him. It is difficult today to remember how bitterly opposed to 'gay' men a large section of the population remained even in the 1980s. His partner was, and is, a quiet, sensitive, shy man who became deeply distressed by the situation.

Eventually Paul's working life became so miserable he was forced to resign. Sadly, he not only left the practice, but also medicine and deprived it of a truly excellent doctor. They left the UK and together founded a hotel business in the USA. We still exchange Christmas cards.

Looking neat and correctly dressed was, in my view, important. (Oh, dear, how would I have fared today?) I still think it is, and cringe to see doctors in their jeans and crumpled open-neck shirts with rolled-up sleeves. (Yes, I know I'm old-fashioned!) Back in the 1960s hospital consultants were often still dressed in pinstripe trousers and black jackets. Almost all the trainees we had respected my wishes – except Danny. Granted, he did travel by motorbike – but apart from changing boots for trainers when he arrived at the surgery, he just shrugged his shoulders and informed me he had nothing else he could wear. He was an excellent doctor and just about faultless in every other respect. One Monday morning he came in looking very, very much smarter than before. After waiting for me to remark on the transformation, he handed me a letter he had received from an elderly patient. Looking rather sheepish he watched me read it. She emphasised how nice he was, but she did find his footwear not what she would expect from her doctor.

She wrote how she found it was hard to think of him as a 'proper' doctor when she looked at his feet. He gave me a grin and displayed a perfectly shod pair of feet. One short letter achieved what I had been striving for months! He earned my great respect. He had a nasty motorbike accident, breaking his leg in two places. I expected him to take a lot of time away – but no, within a week he had organised transport and though, unable to do visits, he manfully did a long day's work in the surgery.

I had a rather similar experience. Trousers, or rather slacks as they were then called, for women, were not generally approved. Offices would send employees home to change. Unimaginable these days when almost all women wear trousers some, if not all the time. Night visits entailed getting out of bed and getting dressed – often in a hurry. It was winter and bravely I had bought a pair of woollen slacks with a view to quicker dressing. Almost the first time I wore them it was to visit a very sick lady in the early hours of the morning. It was made apparent this was not acceptable dress. The middle-aged husband eyed me up and down as he opened the door while enquiring whether I really was the doctor. She spent at least a minute staring at my navy-blue outfit before letting me near her.

We also had students from the local teaching hospital, usually for a fortnight or so, to sit in with us and learn a little about general practice. So often these young people would arrive dressed in clothes looking like unselected items from a jumble sale. Their first morning was wasted having to return home to change into something presentable. But successive students gradually got the message. The medical school Dean rang me irritably explaining what I already knew – students had few funds for smart clothes. But things did improve.

Time off for sickness, maternity leave, paternity leave, compassion leave etc., is all now part of the nation's expectations. GPs, most especially the women, of my generation had to manage without any of this. For many years male GPs preferred not to employ or take women into partnership for this reason. It remains incredibly difficult to arrange cover or reorganise the duty roster at short notice without causing great inconvenience to patients and doctors. There is no way a break in patient cover is possible. Emergencies have to be seen. Yes, there are locums to call upon. But they are expensive, often unknown and cannot just fit into an existing pattern of care. There are agencies now which do the night and weekend work, but it can never be quite right from the patient's point of view. A hefty part of my earnings went on live-in and domestic help for my children. When my mother, who lived with us, died in our house just before morning surgery, there really was only me to see those patients already booked. The funeral arrangements had to wait.

Two women doctors doing shared care and shared hours can and does work.

7. Really?

Doris had been diagnosed in her twenties with multiple sclerosis and by the time I knew her she was wheelchair bound and in her mid-fifties. Her father was then approaching ninety. They lived in a bungalow just across the road from the surgery with all the fittings social services could supply to make her life tolerable, including an invalid car for street use as well as an electric wheelchair. She was not particularly demanding as a patient, and we saw little of her other than to get her medical certificates for insurance purposes. She belonged to various clubs for the handicapped and seemed to live a fairly fulfilled life. We often saw her being collected and delivered to her various activities and lunches. Her clothes were beautifully tailored and her make-up invariably immaculate. The hairdresser called weekly. She looked stunning.

One sad December day her father had been shopping, leaving her at home alone. I got a phone call to tell me he had collapsed and died in a local shop. The proprietor knew her well as she and her father were regular customers. She thought it wiser for me to tell Doris rather than to go herself, or let the police break the news. Quite rightly; also, Doris's basic needs for essential help were more likely to be obtained through me. It was a particularly cold, sleety and dark evening just before Christmas and I did not relish my task. Social Services could be very elusive when needed. I crossed the road, rang the front door bell, but there was no reply. I could hear the radio blaring loudly, so walked round and tried the back door. It was so dark I could not find another doorbell. Feeling rather worried by this time, I returned and crept over the sodden flower garden to see if there was a big enough gap between the front room curtains. There was a small chink of light showing. As I peered through the tiny gap I got a real shock. I really could not believe what I was seeing. Doris was dancing to the music, twirling round and round with great gusto. Stunned, I stood still for a good few minutes with my feet getting increasingly wet and cold. I banged hard on the window. She stopped, stared at the window for what seemed an age, looking totally bewildered. She must have been aware she had been seen. She walked to open the front door to me. It did not seem the right moment for confrontation, besides which I was totally unable to put the necessary words together. I just needed to break the news to her about her father. No need for Social Services.

We never, ever mentioned her 'illness' from which she had made a 'miracle' recovery. Even the local paper wrote an article about her miraculous recovery. The local club for the handicapped gave a party to celebrate the event. Medical certificates were discontinued. She eventually found occupation with the local opticians as a receptionist. No doubt today she would have undergone a huge amount of counselling and probably never worked again. I still have no idea how I really should have handled the situation.

In a totally different category was one of my most lovely patients who had multiple sclerosis. Audrey had been a vivacious teenager, tall, slim with long fair hair and of Nordic appearance. Dancing had been her passion too. It was after a couple of unexplained falls on the dance floor she first came to see me. At that time there was no MRI (magnetic resonance imaging) scans to help with the diagnosis, nor any blood test. After a few months when the falls became more frequent the suspicion it might be this dreaded degenerative disease began to take shape. She saw a consultant who confirmed my suspicions. The disease advanced unusually rapidly and she became housebound.

I looked forward to my monthly visits, but as she worsened in health I almost always came away in tears. She was happily married to a real saint of a man and had a daughter rather unexpectedly. Pregnancy, or the possibility of one, had escaped theirs and my attention. As she had lost the use of her legs by then, and her body was weak, the birth was absolutely without warning, quick and painless. The baby was born at home three weeks before the expected date when she would have been in hospital awaiting the event. Tracy brought both of them great joy, though it left her more disabled than ever. Family, friends, and extra allowances enabled the child to live at home for the first two years of her life. After that, her days were spent in a day nursery and she was collected by her father and brought home in the evenings. It was at about this time Audrey taught me one of life's most important lessons which I have never, never forgotten. There was a flu epidemic in progress and to say I was rushed off my feet would be an understatement. I flew in to see her, intending to make it a very brief visit instead of the usual sharing of a pot of tea. In her slow, slurred speech she asked me to put the kettle on. Slightly impatiently, I explained for the second time how far behind I was and how much I wished there were thirty-six hours in the day, then I would have had the time to make the tea. She looked at me sadly and told me how much she wished there were only twelve hours in a day as they seemed to last forever. I have never again wished for a thirty-six-hour day.

Audrey lived until Tracy was about seven years old. Her father remarried a couple of years later, again very happily.

8. Dogs

Only once in all my years of home visiting did I get bitten – and that was by a Sheltie who knew me well, and used to enjoy a pat on the head during my visits to his piano-teaching owner. It was really her chronically sick widowed sister who required my regular visits. Miss Smith had been fit until she started having attacks of angina a short while before. Both were into their eighties. The house was thick with dirt and dust with an overwhelming smell of dog. I often wondered how the piano pupils managed to concentrate, though, like me, I imagine they got used to the smell. Miss Smith died from a heart attack. I went to give the death certificate to her disabled sister. As I walked through the door, having opened it without knocking, in my usual way, the dog took a chunk out of my hand – no doubt holding me responsible for his owner's death!

How, on another occasion I remained unhurt, still surprises me – and a number of other people too! In the middle of a surgery a voluble Italian burst into my consulting room, having run the gauntlet of the receptionists. The patient sitting in the chair was mercifully fully dressed. The intruder came round to my side of the desk and started to pull me after him. From his distressed state and hysterical Italian it didn't take much imagination to see he wanted me urgently to go with him. I grabbed my visiting bag, apologised to the surprised patient still sitting there with her mouth open, and followed him at a run across the road to where he lived on the fourth floor of a Victorian semi-detached house. Breathlessly I hurried up the stairs after him. His wife was having a miscarriage and, rather unusually, bleeding very, very profusely. Urgently I scribbled a note for him go back across the road to ask the receptionist to call for an immediate ambulance and to give him my emergency bag. That contained the necessary syringes and drugs. I was left alone with the patient – and an Alsatian dog. The dog kept putting its huge head under my arm. I gave him the odd acknowledgement and pat after which he would put his head under my other arm. Desperately I tried to stem the flow of blood but without proper equipment and injections I could do little. What seemed like hours later, but was probably ten minutes, I decided I would have to leave the patient and fetch the things myself. As I got to the top of the stairs, I saw at the bottom two ambulance men, the husband holding my emergency bag and several other members of the household staring upwards. I yelled at them to come up fast. When I quietened down enough to listen I understood they were all scared of the dog! Feeling incredibly angry, I took his collar and led him down the stairs and shut him in the first room I came to. Everything then swung into action and the poor woman got to hospital just about in time to save her life. The dog, it turned out, was a vicious guard dog about to go on very special duty and had deliberately not been fed for thirty-six hours. This, I learnt is normal practice to keep the dog fully alert on duty – it is duly compensated when it finishes work. Only the husband could normally handle him, and the rest of the family were petrified of it. Needless to say, I never went there again unless the dog was shut up.

Dogs were of course in many of the houses I visited. Fortunately I like dogs, but one house to which I had a key always caused me to hesitate before unlocking the front door. The elderly lady had had a stroke and was unable to leave her bedroom. Her son and his wife were out at work all day. It was a large detached house surrounded by tall trees with a dark and dismal hall. There were three Great Danes there. They would emerge slowly – often from different rooms and came to 'greet' me. They were perfectly harmless, but it was very intimidating to have three large dogs all sniffing my face before turning round to continue whatever they were doing before I arrived.

On many occasions I was immensely grateful to a particular dog we owned. She was a cross between an Alsatian and a Doberman, rescued by our local dentist from a tiny flat high up on a council estate. She was the soppiest dog we have ever owned, but when she greeted anyone she showed her long canine teeth and looked incredibly vicious and frightening. As a lone woman doing night visits I felt vulnerable, particularly as year by year it got increasingly dangerous to do so. My instructions to patients requiring late visits were to shut their pets up. I *would* be bringing my dog with me. As you can imagine this was greeted in many different ways – even the allergic-to-dogs patients had to put up with Jessie-dog. Visiting some of the sink estates and high-rise flats was intimidating enough in daylight, but at night with druggies sitting on the iron staircases between the floors and the drunks trying to get up the stairs it was menacing. Oddly enough these people were scared stiff of the dog and gave me a wide berth. If only they had known how useless was Jessie-dog! I'm glad they didn't.

On only one occasion were we in real danger. It was 3 a.m. We were walking back to the car having finished the visit when rocks were thrown at us by a gang of boys. We escaped unhurt, but the car got a huge dent in the rear door. Soon after this event I would only do late visits with a driver – usually my husband but other friends also offered their services. Now, the norm is to have a professional driver for all out-of-hours home visits.

*

Mr G was a recent widower who was finding life unbearable without his wife of fifty-five years. He flopped down into the patient's chair and looked at me with tear-filled eyes. Please, would I give him something to finish him off so he could be with his wife? He sobbed and I wept with him. They had no children, few friends and had been all in all to each other. Eventually I asked him if he would promise to get my prescription made up. He nodded.

Rx One dog to be walked three times a day.

Without looking he took the script. Whether it got as far as the pharmacy I have no idea. About six weeks later he came in clutching a scruffy middle-aged mongrel. It was a rescue dog. They had obviously 'bonded'. Life, he admitted, was possible. He had made so many new friends walking their dogs and with two others he now had a beer in the local pub every lunchtime.

9. Babies

Even as a student I loved seeing or delivering babies. Liverpool Road Maternity Hospital in London is long since demolished but gave both medical and midwifery students superb training. It was incredibly busy, both in numbers and complications. Immigrants poured into the area, many with malnutrition, tuberculosis or other diseases as well as pregnancy. Many could not cope with our sort of diet, or the weather. It was long before the days of ethnic food shops. But, on the whole they liked fish and chips, baked beans and oranges. Nutritionally this was a good diet for a pregnant mother avoiding the dangers of anaemia and vitamin deficiencies. The book and early TV series 'Call the Midwife' records an era only a few years before my time. As students we sometimes accompanied the professional midwives on their home deliveries. A huge eye-opener to most of us. Yes, they did put newly delivered babies into drawers, often with just a very old blanket until social help arrived. Sometimes water had to be fetched from the communal tap. Almost always there were neighbours clamouring to help.

After qualifying I did hospital posts dealing with obstetrics and gynaecology as a special interest. As a junior doctor one was 'on call' for all emergencies as well as in the delivery room. Abortion at that time was illegal (until 1967), so many women and girls in their desperation sought the back-street abortionists with disastrous results. It was heartbreaking trying to save their lives, not always successfully. We were not always able to discharge them, even after extensive surgery, with the hope of having children in the future. Whatever my feelings against abortion were when I started that post, they underwent a change when I listened to some of their stories. Now, abortion is often used as a convenience or instead of being responsible with contraceptives, but then there was much less sexual freedom and if the girl got pregnant in a 'normal' courting relationship it was usual for the fellow to marry her as soon as possible. There were then, and still are genuine, terrible stories of rape (often within the family) as well as abnormalities found on early scans. These (to my mind) warrant abortion.

Yes, I know many of you have strong views on life being paramount. I respect your views. As a GP I have seen so many families founder trying to care for severely handicapped children – yes, again I agree with you, the child is happy and does well until the parents can no longer care for him or her, but the knock-on effect on family and siblings can be serious. No, this book will not enter into the debate – but I do see the other view clearly too.

The Maternity Unit in which I worked for my GP patients was in the central city area and again incredibly busy. All the normal deliveries were done by the midwives, who were (and are), extremely highly trained and skilled. The doctors dealt mainly with the ones that either went wrong during labour or needed forward planning for procedures like caesarean sections. Forceps are used when the baby's head gets stuck. Sometimes this is due to the passageway being slightly tight, or the baby showing signs of distress (this is known by hearing the baby's heart beating either too fast, too slowly or irregularly), or when the mother is too tired to push the baby out, or again if the head is twisted at the wrong angle. The birth canal is oval rather than round. So is the baby's head. During labour the head should rotate to fit the outlet. The skill in using forceps is learnt slowly particularly if the head is high up.

On one occasion before I had really learnt how to use forceps properly, a forty-one year old mother's baby started showing signs of distress. It was her first, much-wanted baby. For those days she was far older than most mothers to be. I phoned for my senior registrar – she was in theatre dealing with another emergency. I rang the consultant in charge. He was half an hour away. There was little choice but to get on with it. The head was so high it needed special straight forceps. I shall never forget the midwifery sister who talked me through it. She could easily have done the job herself, but would not have been allowed to. All turned out well in the end. One healthy baby and one very happy mum.

When the occasional baby died or was stillborn in hospital, it was deeply distressing. It was these occurrences, oddly enough, that made me decide to become a general practitioner rather than the specialist in obstetrics and gynaecology I had planned to be. It seemed very important to me to know the follow-up. How did a family manage to live with such tragedy? Contact with the patient in hospital is transient.

Of the hundreds of home deliveries I attended, the only one to be born on Christmas Day belonged to a religious sect that did not acknowledge Christmas Day! Having left the festivities and my own Christmas lunch, it seemed so sad.

I had the great good fortune to have a superb midwife attached to the practice – absolutely dedicated and not averse to attending one of 'her' patients on her day off. She rather expected me to do the same! Home deliveries in the second half of the 20th century were slightly frowned upon by the experts. Needless to say, there were many mothers who chose, even against advice, to have their babies at home. And also a goodly number who never had time to reach the hospital! The ideal at that time, and now, was for the baby to be born safely in hospital and to go home almost immediately. We GPs did have the use of hospital beds until the economies set in – now few do.

There are few experiences more pleasing than watching a mother hold her baby for the first time. The baby is inevitably messy and not attractive to anyone else. Every time it brought a silly grin to my face. By far the most babies are wanted babies. Sometimes there can be surprises despite scans that reputedly pick up defects. One really sad one I have never forgotten. A solicitor and his wife had prepared everything for their much-wanted baby. They were

Caucasian white parents. The baby arrived dark-skinned and with African features. This couple were well known as friends, as well as patients, and not in one's wildest dreams could one imagine her with an extra-marital affair. It was long before the days of genetic testing. We had been alarmed at the delivery how either or both of them would react when they first saw the baby. She was silent, but he stormed into the office shouting abuse at all of us. Nothing would make him believe it was his child – we offered blood group testing but he said it would prove nothing. It would in fact have proved only a little but could have offered some reassurance. He refused to have mother or baby back home. They went to live with her mother at some distance, she refusing to communicate with any of her former friends.

In reverse a large, happy Jamaican woman gave birth to a pure white baby with African features. It was her sixth, the other five having been left with her mother in Jamaica. I understood they were all black. She was ostracised by her few friends here but her more educated husband was understanding, knowing that in the history of his island there was a great deal of mixing of the races. None of us can be entirely certain of our own entire hereditary possibilities, and oddities; even the very rare ones can occur a number of generations later if both parents carry the latent genes.

Fortunately now scans usually can predict a Down's syndrome pregnancy. Many mothers choose to go ahead, understanding the difficulties, but knowing a great deal of help is available. There is a huge range in this chromosome disorder – some managing normal schooling, whereas others have other major complications and cannot live very long. Some parents decide they will not be able to cope and opt for abortion. Sometimes severe abnormalities are detected, such as a baby without a skull or brain. Thankfully most women choose not to continue a further six or so months with this knowledge. With genetic testing for diseases such as cystic fibrosis there can be even harder decisions for parents to make. The baby, yes, will be disabled physically but mentally normal. Above all such good progress is now being made with research into this particular disease it may become 'curable' in the near future. My job was to put all personal prejudices aside, make sure the prospective parents understood all the facts to enable the right decision to be made for them.

Some doctors refuse to even discuss the possibility of an abortion with their own patients. They then have to look elsewhere either at an agency or with another doctor. I quite often found myself being the 'other doctor'. It makes little sense to me to unload this sensitive issue onto an unknown (and possibly very pro-abortion) doctor. It does take time to explore the past, the present and future implications. The 'empty arm' misery engulfs many women at about the time the baby would have been born, and needs to be discussed in advance. And how they are to cope with any feelings of guilt. There is sadly an increasing number who use abortion a bit like birth control.

*

The pre-Christmas shopping crush of people and traffic always made me try to talk my way out of visits during these busiest of days. Parking in the urban districts of London is and was a nightmare. On one of those early afternoons came a request for a visit for tummy ache and pain on trying to spend a penny. On questioning it did not sound at all serious – probably early cystitis (a very common inflammation of the bladder). After a telephone chat from a telephone box the husband agreed to cycle over and collect a prescription. Fine, or so I thought! An hour or so later he rang again, very apologetically to say she was now screaming with pain. Having driven somewhat recklessly in and out of the traffic I ended up parking in the middle of her (not too busy) side road. On arrival I could hear her from well outside her basement front door. Several neighbours had collected to see what was going on.

It was an impossibly untidy one-room 'flat' with a miniscule kitchen. I had to crawl over clothes, cushions, trays and goodness knows what else to get near enough to examine the girl. She was lying on a double mattress on the floor. She looked like a child but I believe she was actually seventeen years old. The diagnosis was immediately obvious and the baby was not far from arriving. I yelled at the very frightened partner to get a 999 ambulance and tell them the baby was imminent. He had to find a working telephone box first. It was not a good environment for a delivery. The sink was full of washing up – I ended up with a pudding bowl of lukewarm water and some grubby towels just in time to help the baby into this world. The baby had to remain attached to the umbilical cord until I could find a minute to get to my bag. The ambulance arrived just as I handed mother her little girl.

I'm not sure what reaction I had expected, but she was overjoyed and blissfully happy. So was he. Unbelievably neither of them had in any way suspected she might be pregnant! She was plump, but not enormously fat. They thought she had been taking the pill regularly, but I rather doubted it. The local family planning clinic had, she said, done a pregnancy test some months earlier, reassured her and explained taking the pill sometimes stops the normal monthly period. Perhaps then not quite so surprising the baby could grow without being noticed. Pregnancy tests are not infallible, as many women have found to their cost. For hygienic reasons we let the ambulance take her to hospital, meanwhile alerting Social Services to a new needy family. They asked me my first name and named her after me!

Another baby named after me was a very different story. Pamela had had many problems getting pregnant, several miscarriages and was nearing forty years of age. Her husband was supportive throughout her many visits to hospital and as desperate to have a baby as she was. At long, long last all was going well, she was now overdue and was to come and see me that afternoon. However, I was late for the antenatal clinic for a reason I am still ashamed to admit. As there never seemed to be time to stop for lunch I usually had a bag of apples in the car (I learnt to eat the core as well so as not to make a mess), but on this day I had forgotten to buy any. I made a quick dash home to grab some sustenance. Being in a hurry, I reversed out of our drive slap-bang into a bright yellow removals van making a huge dent in its side – and worst of all, a huge dent and smashed lights on the reverse of my car that was only three days old. The usual barrage about incompetent women drivers followed. By the time we had exchanged insurance details I was so late all the parking spaces at the surgery had gone, including the one with my name on it. Parking in the road was difficult, but eventually, very belatedly, the clinic started.

Well into the afternoon there came a tremendous crash outside in the road. The receptionists would investigate, I knew, so I ignored the noise and problem, if there was one. The next patient was a very tearful and shaken Pamela. She also had a new car, but it was an automatic. She had never driven one before. Having put her foot on the accelerator instead of the brake when parking outside the surgery, she had gone full tilt into the back of my car making it a complete write-off. Distressed for her as I was, it incongruously made me relieved I didn't have to get mine repaired! She was more than a trifle surprised at my calm reaction! My namesake was safely born that evening. I recently attended her wedding!

An interesting sequel to my stupidity was a phone call from the removals company. He started off by being fiercely angry – women drivers etc. I tried to calm him down by saying my insurance company would sort it, and, yes, I was really sorry. He suddenly started laughing and told me there was a warehouse full of yellow panels and he had no intention of claiming anything. How many people have a careless car crash and get away without a stain on their insurance?

10. A Foster Parent

Monica was one of the most exceptional people I ever came across. Possibly *the* most exceptional. She could not have done what she did from the early 1960s to 1985 with the current level of screening. Nor did she work with any of the current guidelines from social services. Fostering is handled very differently today with far more stringent supervision. Whilst recognising the absolute and essential need to do this, there is a sizeable number of young adults around who experienced stability, love and care for the remaining years of their childhood after they had entered her home. She did have resident help with the cleaning and cooking.

After leaving school Monica started as a medical student. Unfortunately she contracted tuberculosis. The next four years were spent in a sanatorium in Switzerland throughout the war. Both her parents were killed in a plane crash during this time. Her only brother married and moved away. Her childhood sweetheart had married someone else. On discharge from the sanatorium she did have a little money left to her from her parents. She was not yet fit enough to work full-time. The medical school re-interviewed her, gave her a physical examination and declared her unfit for further study.

Feeling isolated and purposeless she rented a room in central London. For something to occupy her time she started to help out in a charity shop. There were many regulars who either brought in items or bought them. A lot of them were really poor, needing the second-hand clothes, but many others were ordinary people looking for a bargain. Among the sadder ones was a garrulous, smelly, tramp-like elderly lady who was avoided by the other helpers. She really came in for a warm place and a bit of company. Monica felt sorry for her, and possibly having empathy with the woman's apparent loneliness, would take her round the corner for a coffee and sandwich thinking her to be as impoverished as she looked. This continued for many months and eventually the lady died. To Monica's utter astonishment her tramp-like customer had left her a house and a fortune in her will. A true fairy story!

After a lot of thought went into alterations to the huge house. It was set well back in a large garden in my practice area. Once the property was in order she applied to several London boroughs to take in foster children. She would never have passed any medical checks today, but they must have been very rudimentary at best then. Her first family consisted of two boys aged three and one and a sister aged eight. After the father had sat the baby in a bowl of boiling water to stop him from crying the children were removed from their home to be put into 'care'. When the baby was eventually discharged from hospital the children were reunited and placed in Monica's care. Needless to say, they were very disturbed and frightened. Monica had a large double bed. For the first few nights they all slept with her. (How terrible, by today's standards!) Gradually they settled. Other children arrived and for many years she had fifteen or so at a time. Each one had a terrible background, some had spent long periods in hospital recovering from abusive parents and all were disturbed. They were all shown huge love and endless patience. On arrival the task to reach out could seem impossible. I was required to carry out a medical on all admissions and many formally at six monthly intervals. Asthma, epilepsy, eczema, bedwetting and nightmares were common.

Two brothers of Turkish origin, about six and eight years of age, arrived, who had lived like animals in a locked room. My visit times often coincided with their lunch. Grace was always said. The first time I saw these two they had grabbed the plates on either side of them, gulped the food immediately in front of, mouths down, straight off the plates like animals. Then, before there was time to think they grabbed their neighbours' food as well. Monica calmly calmed down the yelling ones who had been deprived of their meals, and served out further helpings before doing a rescue act. A couple of weeks later these two were using spoons and forks just like the others.

A memorable occasion was a Christmas Day when a nine-year-old took the turkey from the kitchen and buried it in the sandpit! Fortunately several of us had gone in to distribute toys and goodies and they all ended up with a good Christmas lunch. That was the one and only time I ever saw Monica in tears and unsure how to cope.

Several of the children had prostitute mothers. One pair had never been out of their cot when found aged somewhere between two and four. The state of their cot defied description. The 'client' had left the prostitute and was looking for a loo. Accidentally he opened the door and recoiled hastily from the smell.

He then thought he heard a whimper and opened the door again, wider this time and saw the two children tied by string in the cot. The cot was filled with excrement, sour bottle of milk, crusts of bread and two filthy children covered in sores. Both spent months in hospital being treated for severe malnutrition and scarring. One eventually recovered fairly well with Monica's care, the other sadly did not. Eventually she had to be placed in a special home. She never learnt to communicate.

A three-year-old daughter of another prostitute would curl up in corners talking to herself. When Polly was asked what game she was playing, would reply she was, of course, playing sex. Her mother visited fairly frequently, keeping in some sort of touch with her daughter. When Polly reached the age of five Social Services thought mother was ready to manage a home visit. She duly was collected by mother and taken to her home in Soho. A couple of evenings later a commuter patient came in to see me at evening surgery. He was clutching a copy of the Evening News. There was a huge picture of Polly on the front page asking if anyone knew this child. Obviously, I did. With the patient's permission I borrowed his paper and contacted the police on the number given. Polly was not stupid, but had promised mother she wouldn't say who she was. Besides she was petrified. Apparently Mother had taken her to her usual soliciting position in Piccadilly, found a client and told Polly to wait until she came back. Fortunately the police found her first.

Another eight-year-old came covered in cigarette burns placed at about one-inch intervals over her entire body. She could only say one of her uncles did it. 'Uncle', being the name given to any of her mother's regular clients. Paedophilia was not headline news in the 1970s and 80s when Monica had her foster home. It was not part of our training nor on our radar. We must have missed dozens of cases, if not more. The stories of these children are endless and made one ashamed to be part of the same human race as their parents.

Monica also found time to run a Guide company, take an active part in church activities and organise a band of volunteer 'aunts and uncles' for the children in her care. Her own health improved rapidly and for many years was trouble free. As she got older she preferred to keep on the younger ones until they became teenagers and gradually reduced her numbers. Every child was followed up after leaving her care. The gap between finishing education, leaving care and adulthood was (and still does) leave many youngsters with huge problems emotionally, socially and job wise. We did try to put Monica up for an MBE but it never actually happened. Almost certainly she would have refused to take it. After the last of the youngsters left her she sold the enormous house and moved into a flat, but even by then Alzheimer's was taking over and sadly she finished her days in a home. We had several children's homes in the practice, but gradually children in need now go into more individual care.

We also had a mother and baby home, especially for schoolchildren. These were heartbreaking in so many ways. For some legal reason at that time under sixteens had to keep their babies with them until they could be adopted at six weeks. By then, many, even the twelve-year-olds had bonded with the babies having fed, nursed and changed them for six weeks. The future care of those babies was hard to envisage. Fine whilst small, but what about the terrible twos? What about the time when the mother wants free time to go out, enjoy herself and find a (hopefully) more permanent partner? Not many of the ones in the home had remotely supportive parents. Not infrequently it was the father or step-father responsible for the pregnancy in the first place. Often it was a case of history repeating itself.

11. Young Men in Trouble

Early on in my career I had a very frightening experience. In fact, it was terrifying. I learnt a great deal from it that stood me in good stead for the rest of my working life. My inexperience made it ten times worse than it should have been.

Mark was the only son of a delightful, typically orthodox, middle-class couple. I cannot remember his father's occupation, but mother with her cheerful smile and sense of fun taught at the local primary school and was well loved by pupils and staff alike. They lived in a spacious semi-detached house with a tree-lined garden in a very quiet suburban road. Mark was in his first year at university reading engineering. It was about 2.30 a.m. Mother rang in great agitation to ask for an urgent home visit. The key, she told me in her panic, was in the door, and please would I let myself in. This should have alerted me to ask just a few questions. It didn't.

However urgent the call for help, it was always wise to know what the problem actually was!

I grabbed my bags, including the one with all the various medications and injections that might be needed, expecting to be able to cope with just about anything. They lived not far from my home. From receiving the call to arriving at their house cannot have taken me more than fifteen minutes. It never took me long to dress. Suitable clothes were always laid out the night before. Dutifully I turned the key, and walked into the small hall announcing my arrival as I did so. The three downstairs doors were all closed, but a muffled voice from the kitchen told me he was in the dining room. I still didn't stop to think why they weren't with the patient. Stupidly, I opened the door into what I correctly judged to be the dining room. I was confronted by six foot plus of a completely mad naked youth at a distance of about eighteen inches. Within seconds he got between the door and me. With hindsight, and really at the time, I never thought he would actually attack me. Then I was in a state of pure panic trying to work out any possible escape route. He was ranting and raising his glazed eyes to the ceiling, appealing to God to help him. I just stood like a dummy not daring to move a muscle. Keep calm, I told myself. Talk to him.

When I could breathe a little more normally, tentatively and in a very conversational tone I tried to discover what he wanted God to do. He stopped his agitated movements to stare at me. God, I was informed in an authoritative voice, refused to let him rest. He had a mission to carry out. He had to keep moving. Rather desperately I told him God had sent me to help. God really did want him to rest before carrying out this important mission. I was sent by God to give him some capsules. Meanwhile I frantically thought through the various sedatives in my bag wondering which would be strong enough to calm him down, should he agree to take them. Eventually, what seemed like an eternity later, he relaxed a little, seemed to accept the idea and asked how I would do it. Would, I asked, he take some blue capsules (Sodium Amytal) if I gave them to him? Eyes to heaven, arms upraised). No, after much consultation with God, blue was not acceptable. Try again. How about red capsules? (Seconal). More arm up-raising and eyes to heaven. No, God did not agree with this either. Sweating by now, in desperation I suggested blue and red ones (Tuinal). Yes! Bingo! God said he could take four. Rather alarmed by the number, but relieved at any possible window of escape, I sat down on the floor, opened my case and selected four capsules. He bent down, grabbed them from my hand and swallowed them ceremoniously without water. A good half hour later during which time he muttered incoherently, while I just sat silently on the floor, he slumped in a heap, deeply asleep.

His parents were quivering outside the door. I could have done with a little help! They, too, had been terrified of their son. Earlier that night they had chased him, stark naked, down their road, worried the neighbours might still be awake and call the police. Actually, that would have been the sensible solution. Mark would have been quickly hospitalised without the nightmare of fuss I encountered.

My next move was to call the duty Mental Social Worker to get Mark admitted to hospital. It was, and still is essential to have two signatures on a compulsory order (a Section) to admit a patient to hospital. Now a relative can be one, but a doctor or qualified mental social worker must be the other. Then it had to be a specialist mental social worker. The chap who came was new to the job and refused to admit him until he could talk to the patient. A more experienced worker would have accepted the history and got on with it. Completely exhausted I left, instructing the parents to phone the minute he stirred. It was 2 p.m. the next day before Mark woke up – the Social Worker who came then had no hesitation in admitting him. This turned out to be a one-off episode. He was discharged about two weeks later and never looked back. He became a very successful engineer.

Drugs obviously were around at the time, but few of us had any experience with them. It never occurred to me Mark might have been experimenting with one of the hallucinogenic drugs. I have never asked. My thoughts at the time were leaning towards a diagnosis of schizophrenia. This often manifests itself at this age in university students. It is a terrible diagnosis. Even with a lifetime of medication, few ever achieve their potential, often becoming social outcasts. They hear voices, receive imaginary instructions and visualise unreal images that they frequently find terrifying and disturbing. Medication offers great relief from the symptoms, but has such unpleasant side effects the patient often wants to stop taking them or avoid the fortnightly injections. The relapses can be disabling. Almost all are now managed in the community, either individually or in hostels. Some, of course, manage outwardly normal lives.

One young lad who really broke my heart came from a very poor background. He virtually brought himself up among his half dozen siblings and totally inadequate parents. The school recognised he was considerably brighter than most. Also, he loved music. He was introduced to a trumpet at the age of eleven, and progressed rapidly, eventually gaining a place at the Royal Academy to read music at eighteen. One of my main interests is music. Any youngster with talent excited my involvement and encouragement. He played in several bands to get experience and earnt a little money. Someone, somewhere offered him an LSD tablet. And he took it. When he confessed it was the only the one he ever took I had no reason to disbelieve him. Sadly he was one of the few people who reacted to this hallucinogenic drug by developing acute schizophrenia. Yes, it is not unknown for this to happen after a single dose. He spent months in hospital after his first severe episode. He never made a sufficient recovery to continue his studies, nor did he ever touch his trumpet again. Last time I had any contact with him was when asked to do a medical report for a hostel in Brighton.

During my working life I must have seen a dozen delightful young people have their lives – and their families' lives – destroyed by schizophrenia. We also had a young man who did take enough LSD to think he could fly. He tried, and it ended fatally with a smashed skull and broken neck.

12. The Slow Ones

This is the one field of care that in my (almost lone) opinion, was much better managed in the middle of the last century than it is today. There were many hospitals then responsible for the care of the mentally handicapped, whereas there are none today. One vast hospital was responsible for our catchment area, necessitating occasional visits from the GP to discuss possible discharge from the hospital. It was a happy place. There was a large warm swimming pool, several shops, a cinema and a massive dance floor occupied most of the day with a noisy band and a great deal of gyrations. There was an army of nurses, teachers, gym instructors, swimming instructors and above all volunteers. Mostly the patients were residents. Many had Down's syndrome. Some had other genetic disorders, some never fully developed; had been just too premature, childhood meningitis among some of the causes. Patients could come by the day, though mainly they were resident. Above all, they could go about freely, shop without being laughed at, be noisy, incontinent or uncontrolled. Most important of all, they had like-minded friends. Yes, we all know how important the individual is, how much better people flourish in small groups, and how much better it is to have a mix of normal and handicapped as both benefit from association with the other. And, yes, the buildings were more like Victorian workhouses than hospitals, incredibly draughty in winter and virtually impossible to maintain. The land on which this hospital stood was valuable and is now a vast housing estate providing living accommodation for thousands. Enough! I remain proved wrong.

We had one of the first groups discharged from this hospital in the same road as where the surgery was. They were placed in a delightful house with an excellent non-resident carer. Four middle-aged ladies. It looked ideal at first. Unfortunately, also in our road was a rather rough secondary modern school. The poor ladies were mocked unmercifully every time the boys encountered them. Eventually they learnt to avoid going to and coming from home at school times. They did unfortunately look different. One of them dribbled. One was very short sighted and had to hang on to one of the others. None of them spoke clearly, or had any real understanding of the value of money. Sometimes their clothes were put on back to front. When they tried to spend their money in the sweet shop the children would stand and stare at them. The parents would then try to pull them away. There was not much to occupy them at the weekends leaving them with little alternative but to wander the streets. They did attend some sort of day unit two or three times each week. We, in the surgery, felt immensely sorry for them. Also found it hard to understand those who found these people so difficult to accept in the community. Often the ladies found refuge in our waiting room. Eventually they did settle, and we all got used to their wanderings, but I remain convinced they were happier in the hospital with plenty to do.

Most handicapped children used to be 'hidden' in special institutionalised homes. Fifty years on it is far commoner for them to be loved and looked after in their own homes. Many attend normal schools and activities where there are trained assistants to help. When this policy was first implemented we got the impression care of the mentally slow was at the expense of the rest of the class and the brightest pupils. There are still 'special' schools, but only for those few who cannot be managed in normal ones. However good the educational, social and health care available, there is a very big price to be paid by the families who care for their own.

Jessica was born not only with severe Down's syndrome, but with a serious heart defect. She was not expected to live much beyond the first two years of her life. The two problems often go together. She was the third child, several years behind the first two. The parents were determined to take Jessica home to give her all the love they could in her anticipated short life. At first the older two rather enjoyed fussing this placid happy baby. After a while when the baby showed no signs of growing up, helping palled. They too would have liked more of their parents' attention. Jessica was not a demanding baby in any way, but her over-protective mother could not bear to leave her alone. The Health Visitor became increasingly concerned as the previously normal, tidy house was becoming more and more untidy with toys and washing everywhere. Meals appeared to be perfunctory, and she could see no evidence of any outings or interest in the older two siblings. Jessica showed little signs of dying, and indeed seemed to go from strength to strength. We did energetically attempt some intervention, but it was to no avail. None of us was surprised when father suddenly took an overseas job and virtually left home. Nor were we surprised to hear both the older ones had major behaviour and learning problems at school. No, there was no happy ending to this saga. Jessica lived until she was almost sixteen, by which time both the older ones had left home. One of them has never to my knowledge made contact again with their mother. The other girl after Jessica died did come home. I guessed she had been living on the streets. I never heard if the father returned.

In a way this was an extreme case, but in every home with a seriously disabled child there is pressure upon every member of that family. It is rarely possible for Mother to go out to work, or to follow a previous career. In the present climate, when so many families need a double income, this can create financial pressures. Then there is the social side. Babysitters are not all willing to sit with a dribbling, floppy baby or a child who keeps falling over and is unable to communicate. As the child grows into a teenager it becomes increasingly difficult for siblings to invite friends to their house. At the other end of the scale I remember one family who lived in a two-up, two-down terraced house with four children. The youngest had Down's syndrome. He was possibly more able than many with this genetic disorder, and even attended a normal school until he was eleven. He was idolised by the whole family and made life richer for all of them.

There remains the decision to be made as the parents and the child get older. For many years their 'freedom' is severely curtailed – often without any resentment. Now so many handicapped live to a good old age there must come a time when the carers need to look elsewhere for care. Is it best to carry on until old age? Or perhaps ill health necessitates an urgent placement? Or is it better to make the change when the child leaves school so he or she can integrate into a lifelong new environment? (There are, for instance, some wonderful farms that are worked by the mentally handicapped.) Or is there a midway better choice? There is no right answer. Over the years many such families would come to talk it over in the surgery. The various agencies did a wonderful job in offering all the alternatives and spending time discussing them with the carers. But I had known these families well, often from the birth of the handicapped baby, and, hopefully, could offer another point of view.

The other common disability that may or may not be associated with low intelligence but is often not – is cerebral palsy. Some are so disabled they need total care in every possible way. Others learn to walk and feed themselves and may indeed grow up to lead independent lives. Cerebral palsy is usually the result of a premature or difficult birth causing damage to an underdeveloped brain. Many are epileptic as well. Jenny was one such born to a happy family with older brothers and sister. She was never able to walk, talk or feed herself and needed twenty-four-hour care. She never grew larger than a seven-year-old and a lightweight one at that. But she could smile and loved having animals and people around. They owned a donkey which spent hours nuzzling her. The dog would sleep in her bed. This was another mother who coped admirably with two other children as well. She raised large sums for charities, included Jenny in all things, cared for unwanted animals and never, ever complained. I knew this family really well. They had a number of problems other than Jenny. I never ceased to admire them and the way they coped. We were all painfully upset when Jenny died at the age of twenty-three.

13. Sick Children

Old people die, often they get ill and then die. Sad, but inevitable. It will happen to the longest living and best of us. Seriously ill children are tragic and very different. Fortunately such events are not common; but every general practitioner will have dealt with a dozen or two in a working lifetime. Often it is the GP who will have the initial suspicion, instigate the necessary investigations and refer to the appropriate hospital. There are occasions when it is the mother who will insist the child is not as before and she knows something is wrong. A golden rule for all doctors is to listen to the complainant! Children are forever getting ailments that end up in the surgery – sore throats, headaches, sickness, rashes and anything else you can imagine, all needing to be seen, diagnosed and possibly treated. It is not surprising the occasional serious diagnosis is missed. Perhaps more surprising, how rarely it is missed. Why should that messy throat not be an ordinary infection? Why should that nervous child not have ordinary headaches? I mentioned the sixth (or should it be seventh?) sense which doctors develop. Probably a result of a detailed five years' study at medical school, several years in hospital wards and exposure to general practice all being somewhere available in one's computerised memory.

One such was an older child who was frequently being brought to the surgery with his fussy mum. The sore throat didn't look all that out of the ordinary, but he did look a bit pale. For some reason I ordered a blood test. With hindsight I still cannot think why I did. Possibly to show Mother I was doing something? He was in hospital that evening with acute leukaemia. Eventually he had a marrow exchange organised by Great Ormond Street and made a full recovery. I still wake at night worrying what would have happened if the extra sense had not kicked in.

Every doctor dreads missing meningitis. Hopefully with newer vaccines there should be much less of it around. Every child at some stage gets a high temperature and a headache. Few with meningitis get the classic rash on their tummies. It's not the easiest of diagnoses and I admitted one or two who turned out not to have the disease, but thankfully managed to never miss one that did.

Now we have scans there are far fewer babies born with spina bifida and or hydrocephalus. The first is a gap in the spine letting the vital spinal cord fluid, occasionally the spinal cord itself and coverings bulge out – the degree varies from causing just weakness in the legs to complete paralysis. Hydrocephalus is caused by the circulation of fluid round the brain being blocked, and not being able to drain away the head swells to gigantic proportions, squashing the brain. Hydrocephalus used to be a death sentence before the first birthday. Now a simple operation can install a drainage system. It is still not possible to relieve all cases of spina bifida.

Samantha had spina bifida. Her legs were totally paralysed and she had no control over her bodily functions. I first met her when she was three years old in her push chair with a huge smile on her face. She was a little slow in her mental development, but by the age of five could attend the local school where she rapidly became everyone's favourite. She had such a happy disposition. The children clamoured to push her chair and to sit next to her. The staff loved her. What her future would have held, I cannot guess, but one of her frequent waterworks infections caused kidney failure and she died. I have rarely seen so many attend a funeral. It was even more tragic than usual as she was an only child.

Another poignant death was in a baby whose disease should have been picked up by one of us somewhere along the line. It was mother who brought her in asking if the funny appearance of the eye was normal. The pupil looked hazy, rather like an older person with a large cataract. Sadly it was a rapidly growing aggressive cancer. Short of removing the eye before the disease had spread elsewhere there was little then that could be done. That would have been long before the hazy appearance of the pupil. Now there are treatments for this – often successful. New-born babies are medically examined soon after birth and again at about six weeks of age. They have frequent visits for immunisations and examinations throughout their first few years but I'm still not sure I would have looked for that particular disorder. Needless to say afterwards I always did, but never met another case.

Heart surgery has become so commonplace now, and on the whole comparatively safe, it is easy to forget how risky any such intervention was even a few years ago. Carol was a beautiful baby almost from the day she was born. Much wanted and much loved. Her parents were affluent and gave her everything she needed. Carol had long, fair Scandinavian-type blonde hair, blue eyes and a happy disposition. She grew tall and slim with an enviable figure. Her heart murmur was noted soon after birth, was investigated, but not then regarded as particularly serious. Mother never fussed, and when she brought Carol to the surgery at the age of five complaining of her breathlessness I took her seriously. Carol's lips did look just a little bluer than expected but she was unconcerned. Many holes between the two halves of the heart heal spontaneously as the child matures. Carol's had not, and indeed had grown larger, causing the unoxygenated blood to mix with the oxygenated blood, giving an inadequate circulation of good red blood to her body. There were other heart abnormalities too. Over the next few years she was seen by numerous heart physicians and surgeons. All at that time were reluctant to recommend surgery. Gradually she became unable to walk even short distances. Her life was distressingly limited. Just before her sixteenth birthday she asked to accept the risk to have surgery. She was fully aware of the possibility of not surviving the operation, and tried to prepare her parents (and the rest of us) for this eventuality. Carol herself was cheerful and had made all her preparations for dying. So sadly, after an eight-hour operation she did. Not of the surgery itself, but a massive post-operative clot of blood to her brain. Years later her parents and brother were still deeply in mourning, yet to the outside world looked to have recovered. They are such a lovely family. All three had given up their church attendance, not perhaps surprisingly, having lost their faith. How does anyone get used to the loss of a child? In previous centuries the percentage of children not reaching maturity was high and many parents lost several children. How did they cope?

One boy I shall never forget was Joshua. He was asthmatic from birth and if only the resources available today had been available in the 1970s he would still be alive now. But they were not. Ventolin (salbutamol) had just become readily available and gave him great relief. He was using about one a week enabling him to attend school regularly and enjoy time with his friends. To save prescribing time he was given three inhalers together. He was found dead in bed the next morning having used all three inhalers in just one night. The post mortem results did not show clearly whether it was the overdose or the asthma itself which had killed him. Another hugely devastated family. A big lesson learnt for me – to ensure patients really know and can repeat exactly how much and how often medication should be taken. And, the dangers of taking an incorrect dose. Now this duty is largely undertaken by the pharmacist.

A possibly commoner cause of childhood and teenage deaths now, rather than in previous years, is suicide. The media highlights the dangers of bullying, social networking, illicit drug-taking and academic pressures. These may indeed be the causes, but the parents, siblings and all who have come into contact with the young person are filled with guilt. This guilt can never really leave them. With the internet it is now easier for such parents to join self-help groups to get some relief.

14. Anorexia

This enigmatic condition has undoubtedly been around for centuries. One of the most difficult problems to confront the GP. Trying to help an anorectic is a bit like trying to demolish a brick wall with one hand. Once I thought I was on the brink of getting some understanding of a cause for this frightening condition. Also finding an answer to the reason a patient 'recovers' when she or occasionally he, decides to eat again. Recovery is probably not the right word. Most anorectics have a lifelong problem with eating.

Hazel was a fourteen-year-old with anorexia. It was her mother who I sincerely hoped would be able to help me to help others. One day she came alone whilst Hazel was at school. She had, she said, never told Hazel that she herself had nearly died of anorexia nervosa when she was at Cambridge. Currently she taught classics in a local school. At her lowest, she told me, she weighed barely four stone. It seemed unbelievable that this rotund, middle-aged teacher could ever have been so ill. Please, I asked, would she tell me why she had forced herself to starve almost to death? She shook her head vigorously. All she could tell me was it was a form of self-discipline. Being fat was so ugly it had to be stopped. She said she never saw herself as dangerously thin or in a life-threatening condition, only and always as too fat. What, I then asked, had made her eat again? Again she shook her head. She admitted she had no insight whatsoever as to what drove her to it, nor what enabled her to recover. None of the interventions to which she had been subjected, several hospital admissions, psychotherapy or counselling had had the slightest effect on her attitude to anorexia. Undoubtedly the hospital admissions had kept her alive. She qualified the latter by admitting she still had an eating problem, but this now was more in the form of bulimia. Also now how utterly helpless she felt to be any help her daughter. She was very frightened Hazel might become really ill – even die. So, like most before me who have tried to research this condition, I only learnt how ill understood is this disorder. Like so many of them Hazel was highly intelligent (just visit

Oxbridge and see how many are there). By the time she was eighteen she was almost a normal weight and very sensibly decided to attend university in London rather than leave home at that point.

Another patient, Kathleen, did not recover. Her lovely parents pursued every known avenue of help. They were sensible people. After innumerable hospital admissions for intravenous transfusions of fluid and nutriments when on the brink of dying, she eventually at the tender age of eighteen did succumb. I can never forget the utter hopelessness of trying to suggest to her the need to eat, of demonstrating in a long mirror how skeletally thin she was and of trying to break through the barrier of her irrational thinking. To try, with her parents, to remove the hundreds of laxatives hidden all over the house. She took dozens every day. Kathleen remained lucid and articulate until moments before she died. By this time she really wanted to die. I was with her parents when it happened. I knew this family well but could never see any hidden agenda that might have triggered the anorexia. Nor with other families who have had to cope with this illness.

Innumerable articles and books have been written on the subject. One or two hospital units claim to successfully treat anorectics. My experience with referring patients to these special units was that they only admitted the ones who would almost certainly 'recover' anyway; the more serious ones were deemed "unsuitable for this unit". Needless to say Kathleen was in this latter category. It kept their statistics looking good. Mostly one admitted the seriously ill ones to the local hospital, where they would be treated with intravenous nutrition, gastric tubes, encouragement and onward referral to the nearest psychiatric unit. One experiment, I think by the Maudsley hospital in south London, was particularly interesting. They chose a statistically significant number of anorectics and a matched number of normal people. Each person was asked to place two posts as close together as they felt they could safely drive a car between. Normal people left a couple of feet each side of where they thought the car would go. Those with anorexia left a hugely wide gap with several feet each side of the car. Self-image does play a part. High intelligence also seems to be common. Mostly girls are affected but there are boys as well. The one boy I can remember who was a patient, not of mine, but of the practice, died at the age of eighteen.

A headmistress of a local (then) grammar school had a number of anorectics in her upper classes. She sought the help of a skilled counsellor and every lunch time insisted these girls sat with her for lunch and attended daily counselling sessions. It ensured they attended school, also that nutrition was taken at least once a day. One essential is to keep the girl in place so she cannot self-vomit the meal. This programme made it possible to do just that. I have no idea how successful it all was, but it was about the best idea I ever heard of.

There are a huge number of websites for anorectics. Group therapy via the internet is commonplace for today's young. Disastrously most of them are not there to help with eating more food, but the complete opposite. They show ways of losing yet more weight by taking laxatives, excess exercise and how to deceive the outside world.

It used to be a disorder of the mid to late teens and early twenties. Now an increasing number are much younger, some only nine or ten years of age. Sometimes the parents take a long time to realise what is happening. One mother, Sally, had a sudden awakening to the seriousness of her daughter's behaviour. She had been so pleased when fourteen-year-old Mary seemed to grow up and be helpful, after a couple of really stroppy years of non-co-operation. Mary became the first to get up from the meal table to clear the plates and fill the dishwasher.

Her younger sister had tried to tell Sally a lot of food on the plates was going in the waste bin, and she thought it was mostly Mary's. Sally had ignored this as a bit of sibling aggro. Then she had been pleased to see Mary stop wearing what she termed 'minimal clothing' and wear pretty flowing tops and skirts. Also Mary took up running having previously been the most un-sporty of girls. Again Sally was pleased, thinking Mary was getting over the difficult teenage period. The shock came when she accidentally invaded the bathroom just as Mary got out of the shower. In itself that was unusual – anorectics usually are meticulous in locking doors to ensure their privacy. It was the shock that brought her to my surgery door. Her husband refused to believe any of it – not an unusual reaction. Like most mothers she tearfully tried to find out where she "had gone wrong". No doubt some hospital somewhere has a group where mothers can meet and try to thrash out this problem, then hopefully each would realise it had absolutely nothing to do with anything in the upbringing. Of all the consultations I had it was with the patient and the relatives of anorectics I felt most utterly helpless. Mary did survive. Unusually, she was not over bright and I seem to remember went to work in a local supermarket.

The opposite disorder, bulimia, is closely related. It was in the news a great deal when Princess Diana was diagnosed with it. Families end up putting locks on fridges, cupboards and larders. One girl I remember would come down in the middle of the night and demolish an entire loaf of bread as well as cornflakes and pints of milk. No doubt most of it ended up pretty quickly down the pan. The compulsion to eat is just overwhelming, alongside, very often, the need to lose a lot of weight. Some swing from being grossly overweight to being dangerously thin. And, like anorexia, the websites do more to encourage than to discourage the abnormal behaviour. No doubt, one day, probably not too far into the future, they will find a gene to fit these disorders – then it might be possible to get to grips with some effective treatment.

15. Education

Really education had very little to do with my work, but once or twice I got rather involved. In one case I was rather proud of myself. Andrew was a delightful ten-year-old. I got to know him as both of us walked our dogs round the park very early in the morning. We had really interesting conversations ranging round all sorts of topics. I regarded him as one intelligent lad. At no stage did I pick up he was unhappy at school or having any sort of problem with learning. It was with great surprise one evening his mother plonked herself down in the surgery chair and burst into tears. I looked at Andrew who just shrugged his shoulders. He was wearing the uniform of a local prep school, one not exactly renowned for its high flyers. In the past I had been a little puzzled as to why he was at that particular school. When the tears subsided the whole story came out. Andrew had been expelled – yet again. "Why?" I asked in utter astonishment.

The answer was even more astonishing. "Because he cannot learn to read, and they think he should be at a school for educationally subnormal children."

It turned out he had started at the local infant school moving on aged seven to the primary school. There the mother had been called in to see the head who tactfully tried to tell her Andrew needed to be at a special school. He was unable to do the simplest of reading or numerical skills. Angrily she exited the office and marched him home. The parents placed him in a good, well-known, prep school – a thing they could ill afford. Six months later they were asked to remove him from there. Hence the placement in the rather poor school he currently had attended. It did seem odd to me she had never done any reading or writing with him to try and help. Normal parents spend time with their children in the early school years with reading and numbers. I never verified it, but suspected she had exactly the same problem. Later I guessed this must have been the case because Andrew told me it was his father who read him stories. Andrew always had a fund of them to tell me, particularly detailed ones about engines that I never understood.

Dyslexia is well known today – and well understood

how very disabling it can be. Then it was considered to be the middle-class way of explaining away a not very bright child. Having calmed mother down, I gave Andrew a pencil and asked him to write his name on a piece of paper. Left-handedly he put down all the right letters (except the 'd' looked like a 'b') but in a nonsense order. Likewise I asked him to write down a four figure number. Again, correct numbers, but jumbled. Now, I know very little indeed about education, but it did not take great intelligence on my part to diagnose his problem. Surely three schools could not miss the incongruity of his obvious high intelligence and written and numerical problems? But they had. Fortunately I had a colleague who had specialised in language disorders at a London institute that was researching help for dyslexics. I rang her then and there, but, she informed me, there would be at least a six-month wait before Andrew could be seen. I pleaded, exploded and insisted his problem was urgent. She just calmly said there were a lot of children in the same category, and he would have to wait his turn. All I could say to Mother was that I would continue to do my best for Andrew, but just leave it a few days before following up a further, possibly 'special' school.

The next day a miracle happened. My colleague rang to say one of her pupils was moving overseas –

she could see Andrew the next day. He was diagnosed with an exceptionally high IQ, but was suffering from very, very severe dyslexia. Our morning walks continued and I followed his progress with great interest. Within months he had been taught to count and do complicated sums using his knuckles. He learnt the rudiments of reading. He blossomed. After about another six months the institute arranged for him to attend an ordinary secondary school though he still needed a great deal of help. His great desire had always been to be an engineer. I don't imagine he ever was able to enjoy reading a book, but he did go to university and did become a mechanical engineer with an oil company. I look forward to my Christmas card each year – now signed Andrew, Anne and Danny.

Not exactly an educational problem, though this lad got more medical certificates for school and university than any other I can remember. John had rather fussy Scottish parents and a younger sister. The first time I met him was before his sister was born. He was somewhere round a year old. A very, very common consultation, usually dealt with by the health visitor – a feeding difficulty. Our excellent health visitor, Mother told me, was of no help to her. It was no good her telling her to stop giving him mashed potato and to try something new. Or even to put something else in the mashed potato to add some protein. She'd tried a teaspoon of egg yolk in the potato. He just spat it out. In fact he spat everything out that wasn't mashed potato. Having ascertained he still had plenty of milk to drink, that he didn't look remotely anaemic or anything other than a very healthy baby, I told her to stop worrying. Lots of babies and children were fussy eaters, I told her, but grew up perfectly normally with a varied diet. Milk and mashed potato did seem rather short of vitamin C, there being no fruit or vegetable included, but there must have been just enough in the potato.

I never gave John another thought until about a year later when Mother mentioned John was still surviving on mashed potato, though he now liked chips as well. He drank some milk, but much preferred plain water. Slightly alarmed, I asked her to bring him in next time she came. He looked a perfectly healthy, normal toddler, just bursting with chat and energy. Mother claimed she occasionally tried to give him something either off their plate or a treat but he steadfastly refused to try anything else. It was difficult to believe he wasn't getting more of a balanced diet from somewhere. However, I could only reassure Mother he looked fine and send her on her way. The next time it came up for discussion was when he was to start school and needed to stay for lunch. By this time, she claimed, his diet consisted of mashed potato, chips and one sausage a week. He would only drink water. Could she have a certificate for school to explain his diet? Now I was becoming worried my reassurances may have caused a major health problem. I insisted he had a blood test before I would issue a certificate. It was completely normal, again raising my suspicions he was getting a better diet than was described. The certificate was issued. For various reasons John changed schools a few times and each time we had the rigmarole of a certificate to be excused lunches. When he was somewhere around nine years old I tried to have a chat with him. Useless. He only confirmed what he would eat – mashed potato, chips and a sausage a week. As he grew older we had the same discussion I suppose, about once a year. He looked and was fit. He played sport. He shone at academic work. He slept well. Also, as a budding scientist, he became aware of the eccentricities of his diet. But, as he informed me, he was fine. Why should he change? He went on to university and had to live in hall. Another certificate. He is now a professor in the university, living a full and normal life, and, still living on mashed potato, chips, an occasional sausage and water. Please don't try it! It could never work with anyone else.

On the strength of treating, or perhaps not treating this patient I found myself being too relaxed with John. John had a very inadequate and fussy mum. He seemed to be surviving on crisps and sweets. She complained he wouldn't eat properly so many times I got used to automatically telling her to stop worrying. One day I did give him the once over. He was a bit pale. His blood test showed quite severe anaemia. We did adjust his diet! Conscientious middle-class parents can be too careful with diet, forgetting children must have full cream milk, and there is nothing wrong with fun food occasionally. What is suitable for a careful low diet in an adult is not the same for a child.

Some of the very over-bright children do cause problems. I had two such patients at about the same time. Patience was a doctor's daughter attending the local high school. This had a policy of never allowing girls to study other than with their own age group. By the age of thirteen Patience was bored stiff with school. Instead of being her usual top of the class, she ended up at the bottom, with a threat of expulsion hanging over her. That was when my colleague asked me to give her a thorough medical to find out why she was so listless and depressed. Physically she was fine. Mentally, I felt she was so seriously depressed her life was at risk. She could not see the point of living, there was no future, she had no idea what she wanted to do and things like homework were just a waste of time. She used to have lots of friends but now she couldn't be bothered with any of them. Anyway, none of them liked the things she liked. What she did like I could not discover. I didn't dare ask the standard question: "Have you ever thought of doing away with yourself?" (Today it would have been easier to ask this) It might, I thought, have planted a seed to grow into later action. Because she was a friend and colleague's daughter, I felt it incumbent upon me to go further into the problem before asking Father's permission to refer her on to a psychiatrist. I guessed, correctly, this would not be given easily. Instead, I asked if he would give permission for me to speak to the headmistress who, I imagined, must have experience with this sort of problem, and would through the school medical services have a route for referring Patience for counselling or psychiatric help. This would, I hoped, seem far less threatening to the parents. Also the headmistress would be as concerned as her parents and I were. She, when eventually I managed an appointment with this superior lady, absolutely disagreed with me. She would know, she assured me, if Patience was at all depressed. She knew about teenage girls. The girl was just being deliberately defiant and difficult. Venturing to suggest she might not find enough stimulation at school, I got a very angry response. Patience, she informed me, had no more, in fact probably had less, ability than the rest of her class. I tried to suggest, because I had known she could read fluently at the age of three, and by seven had read everything in her primary school, she just might, I ventured, have had a bit of a head-start at the beginning? Normal, I was informed. Lots of girls did that. It was no indication of ability. She might well have been right, but I didn't think so. With no alternative I tentatively relayed my diagnosis to Patience's father. His reaction was not dissimilar to that of the headmistress. There was nothing at all I could do, so I left it alone. It had started, after all, as an educational problem to her parents, not a medical one.

I heard nothing for a couple of years and had almost forgotten Patience's existence. I had avoided her father at medical meetings. The whole business had left me feeling uncomfortable and embarrassed. One evening surgery a mother accompanied by her tearful sixteen-year-old daughter came to ask advice. She was about to sit her GCSEs and was so worried by them she couldn't stop crying. Mother wouldn't, she said, want the same thing to happen to her daughter as had happened to Patience. I raised an eyebrow. She was very surprised I hadn't heard. Patience had taken a huge overdose some weeks ago and was still seriously ill in hospital and was quite unable to sit her exams. No, I didn't feel smug at having been vindicated in my diagnosis. I felt incredibly guilty at not having insisted on her receiving treatment. Patience did survive, but at a cost. She had suffered brain damage. Quite how badly I never discovered, but sufficient for the mother and children to leave Father behind and move well away from the area.

Valerie was a different story altogether. She came from a very uneducated family but obtained a scholarship at the age of eleven to the local girls' public school. Her father was unable to work for several years after a serious accident so when he came for his certificates I was able to ask about her progress. They were so proud of her, but had no understanding of her needs. She did brilliantly for the first two or three years and really shone. Probably making school friends was not easy – she had a very marked South London accent. Her home friends I imagine would have gradually faded, her home life become more isolated and eventually she begged her parents to let her go to the local comprehensive school. After a lot of truanting they capitulated. She ended up as a shop assistant in Woolworths without a single qualification.

16. Home Visits

In the USA and Canada these do not happen. Or at least, not as standard. I sincerely hope we in the UK manage a balance between the patient's needs and sensible use of the doctor's time. Obviously it is possible to see three patients in ideal surroundings in the surgery to one visit at home in possibly an ill-lit bedroom with a bed at a difficult height on which to make an examination. When I first started in practice there were often twenty or more visits in a day. Patients who asked for a visit almost always got one. That was before antenatal clinics, baby and child health clinics, health screening, cervical smears, family planning clinics, minor ops, diabetic clinics, hypertension clinics, old age check-ups etc. were added to the day's work. Now some years later many of these roles have been undertaken by specially trained nurses and midwives. Meanwhile the whole world of treatable complaints has escalated with so much more to investigate, in more and more complicated ways, that there is no way the doctor has any more time for much home visiting. Yet, it can be a hugely important part of patient care.

Stella nearly drove the staff, partners and myself to the brink of being extreme rudeness. She did have four children under six so had plenty of contact with the health visitor, but no, this was not enough and almost every day there she would be in the waiting room, to be seen in the emergency clinic. Usually with all four in tow creating mayhem with the available toys there. Sometimes one of them would have an ear or throat infection but on the whole they were a healthy crew. One morning she rang for a home visit. The receptionist took the phone number and suggested I might like to see if a visit was really necessary before going there. It must have been a fairly easy day because I decided I would visit without bothering to phone first. I am so glad I did. She lived on the second floor of a four-storey block of social housing flats. The lift was, of course, out of action. I was grateful I had only one doctor's bag to lug up the stairs. Shopping for six, I thought, on my way up, would be hell to carry – with the children as well. Particularly as the baby and the two-year-old would need to be carried too. I could hear the toddler screaming from the bottom of the stairs so had no difficulty in locating the right flat. He had a high temperature and severe earache. While I was examining him someone in the flat below was banging on the ceiling with, I supposed, a broom handle. Having quietened the boy a little I asked her what that was all about. She said it happened every time the baby cried or the children played noisily. And, she added, the chap upstairs would stamp on the floor at the same time. On my return to the surgery I asked the health visitor why on earth they could not be rehoused more suitably. It was a three-bedroom flat, I was informed, and a there was a massive queue for houses. Lots of mums, she informed me, were in this situation. However, a few pointed letters and phone calls later and we did get her rehoused to a place with a small garden. There she would not have to lug the push chair up and down all those stairs. The house was not in our area, but I guess the innumerable surgery visits ceased.

Many visits gave exciting and interesting insights 'behind the scenes'. After several years we linked up with another practice to give out of hours cover. It meant only being on call one night in nine and one full weekend in nine. Meant being far more busy, but such a lovely feeling when the duty was over knowing there were eight good night's sleeps in between! We had a theatre in the other practice area and occasionally I was called to see a performer or backstage member of staff to give urgent treatment so the show could go on. Quite difficult on occasions. No-one yet has found a cure for the common cold and I was no exception. However, there were minor remedies available and it was rewarding to meet some of the more famous actors and musicians who visited.

Pubs in the cold light of day are not the warm and welcoming places they are when open to the public. In the morning they reeked of cigarettes, urine, dirt, stale beer and food waste. Treading over this mess and the vacuum cleaners to reach the upper living quarters was always unpleasant. Few publicans lived any sort of normal life and their quarters were almost as bad. It was unusual for them or their wives to be ill at all – they were far too busy.

A large percentage of the practice came from the Indian subcontinent, many having arrived with serious medical conditions. The children soon adapted but were often inadequately clothed and fed for our climate. Needless to say as soon as they started school they caught every minor infection going as they had no natural immunity. The parents were not used to our snuffly complaints, became really worried and asked for visits. I was very impressed by the way they cared for their children. Consultations for difficulties in sleeping are very frequent with our English babies and children. A complaint that keeps health visitors very busy. Not with those from Asia. Babies and children are kept in constant contact and until quite old sleep in the same room as their parents. They think we are barbaric in making a small child sleep in his or her own room. Often visiting one of these children meant climbing over three or four beds first. Behind the scenes in some of the take-aways was so messy I never bought from that place! Regulations and inspections ensure now a safe standard of cleanliness.

Visiting the frail elderly was always rewarding. Yes, they could have had transport to come to the surgery, but that was years after I began. And even in later years there were many I chose to visit regularly. This often prevented an out of hours call to be seen by a doctor not known to them. Some of them had had such interesting lives and I so enjoyed their reminiscences. A few I timed carefully knowing the tea would be ready and a special cake made!

Nursing and care homes always had and have regular visits. Everyone now calls everyone else by their first names. I dislike it intensely, especially when a chit of a girl in a care home calls a very old and frail person in this way. One stands out particularly. She asked 'George' to come for tea after he had seen me. Knowing this dignified man to have been a fleet naval commander I asked whether he had given his permission for her to use his first name. No, he informed me, and he tried to ignore any requests made in this way even if it did make him appear to be deaf or confused. I spoke both to the girl concerned and to the matron but guess they took absolutely no notice. On a personal note I was once a patient in a major hospital. On admission I was asked the usual question as to how I would wish to be addressed. "Doctor or Mrs, please," I requested. (I am always known by my middle name when a first name is used.) The next morning the trolley lady asked very loudly if I would like a cup of tea calling me by my first name which I failed to recognise! So much for admission forms. I suppose I shall have to update my ideas one day – but not yet.

Seeing a patient in his or her own home is always revealing – one never sees that person again in quite the same way. Often it is really helpful. That patient with the intractable back pain can be seen, despite advice in the surgery, sitting in a far too low chair and sleeping on a too soft or ancient bed. The patient with the hopelessly swollen ankles who is not able to get up the stairs and sleeping in an armchair at night. The arthritic patient steadily losing weight with three steps up to the kitchen. Just two steps too far to do more than once a day. The smelly patient with only an upstairs loo. And so much more can be seen. Many independent elderly are less than truthful about the help they get.

Dora used to visit the surgery monthly to sort out her heart failure and blood pressure pills. Always she would tell me about her wonderful daughter who did everything on her frequent visits. The day came when I had to visit her. The house was in disorder, dirty, the washing up half done, the bathroom indescribable and the fridge almost empty. Was, I asked, her daughter on holiday? She burst into tears and told me her daughter was too busy to come more than once a month and she then only stayed for a cup of tea. She had felt so ashamed of this. Like most of the other problems much can be done once the basic problem is recognised. A visit from occupational health can and does provide miracles. A district nurse visit can solve many a medical issue. Carers can be put in place and so on.

We doctors can be a selfish lot! Often we think only

our time is precious. Our practice did try to value the patient's needs a bit. A car can get to a sick child at a distance to the surgery very quickly. A mother with several children, no car and a child with a high temperature has a big problem. A confused elderly patient can be visited at home more easily than by travelling on a bus accompanied by an equally elderly spouse. We started consultations at 8 a.m. for the business or hourly paid who could ill afford time off work.

Visiting a delightful lady recovering from a heart attack we both stood looking out of her bedroom window surprised to see a Scottish removal van taking the furniture out of the house opposite. My patient was not entirely surprised as the two sisters who lived there had spoken of going back to Edinburgh to retire. They were currently up there visiting family. The first van was followed by a second one from the same firm. At this stage I left. Yes, you've guessed correctly. Thieves had stolen every item from that house, including the electric light bulbs. Nothing was ever recovered or the thieves located.

17. The Autistic Spectrum

The condition must have existed for centuries, if not forever. Only in recent years, however, has it been defined and researched in any detail. Asperger's syndrome had no mention in my textbooks, but is commonplace in all classrooms today, by name. There were always the 'difficult' children whose parents, or they, got the blame for their behaviour. Now, we know, it often has a completely different explanation.

Asperger's syndrome is the less severe end of the autistic spectrum. Those at the other end of the scale have no ability to communicate, nor sadly to live any sort of normal life with their peers. We have all been amazed by the lad on TV who could not communicate, read or write but who could, after a brief look, draw every detail of St. Pancras Station with all its minute detail absolutely correct. Another young man who also reached international as well as

TV fame was an exceptionally gifted pianist. The presenter gave an insight into the patience and unusual methods his teacher used to help improve his technique. The young man was, of course, quite unable to read a music score but could retain concertos and sonatas correctly in his memory. A child I know well is now eleven and has at long last been found to be unable to learn in a normal classroom situation, even with one-to-one help. But he can make the most perfect plasticine models of people in miniature with every finger and toe detail perfect. He will be attending a special school next term where his incessant, agitated movement and unrestrained behaviour will not disrupt other pupils who might be trying to learn. It is such a huge step forward over the last decades to see disabled children fully integrated into normal education but there are occasional exceptions. John is one of them.

Perhaps the most interesting discovery of autism, to me, was one of twin boys born to perfectly normal parents. At the age of six months Mother became increasingly concerned by the difference between the boys. Twin one responded, gurgled and smiled at her. Twin two, John, appeared neither to see her nor hear her speaking to him. Various tests showed his hearing and vision to be within normal limits. His physical development was comparable with that of his brother. Referral to the paediatric department of a major London hospital resulted in the diagnosis of autism. He was onward referred to another unit where research was being made into this sad condition. Numerous hospital visits did nothing to improve his behaviour, but brought some comfort to the parents who had begun to believe it was some fault on their part. He was a full-time job for his mother until at school age he was found a suitable (not mainstream) placement. She needed respite care during the holidays. When a surgery visit was necessary she would phone me first, to make sure not only that everything movable in the consulting room was out of reach, but that he could come straight in without encountering anyone in the waiting room or reception. He could move at tremendous speed and tolerated nothing loose on shelves or tables. He was also incredibly strong for his age. By the age of fourteen he was almost six feet tall and could no longer be managed at home. He had become a prize escapologist. Finding a place for him was a nightmare. The local council could offer nothing. Eventually a really excellent home was found in the east of England. Fortunately he settled better than expected in this special unit where he had two carers all the time. His brother was completely normal in every respect and a great joy to his parents.

John was the most severely affected patient I had, but there were others less severely affected who also made their parents' and siblings' lives incredibly hard. Worst, perhaps, in adulthood where the workplace was not for them. Without respite care holidays become impossible, visitors feel unwelcome or embarrassed, siblings cannot easily bring friends home and almost always sleep patterns are deeply disturbed. So often one parent has to give up work. Even more sadly, I have seen more than one marriage unable to survive the strain.

18. Dementia

"Would you like a cup of tea?" was the pleasant way Miss Preston greeted me. I thanked her and said how nice that would be. A few seconds later the question was put again. And again. And again. Through almost the whole of each twenty-four hours it would be repeated at minute intervals. She had taught in a local primary school all her working life, becoming close friends with her headmistress. After retirement they had bought a house together and for some ten years it worked out well. Gradually it became apparent to Miss Lucas her friend was becoming demented. At first she coped patiently, feeling it was her responsibility. After a year or so even leaving the house to shop, or speak to a friend on the phone became almost impossible. The situation had become intolerable. Her friend followed her constantly from room to room and seemed not to need any sleep. How Miss Lucas had tolerated the situation for as long as she did speaks highly of her care and commitment. After just a half hour's assessment and a physical check-up I was finding it almost unbearable to be asked yet again if I would like a cup of tea.

Suitable accommodation at this time was usually in a psychiatric unit. There were few dedicated homes other than in the private sector. The psychiatrist I arranged to visit her had no vacancy then, nor in the foreseeable future. He already had a long waiting list. What to do? Providence somehow stepped in as so often she does when the situation becomes desperate. Miss Lucas fell down the steps outside her front door and fractured her hip. Social Services stepped in at last, and a temporary nursing home was found for Miss Preston. After a prolonged hospital stay for Miss Lucas it was obvious Miss Preston could not possibly return home. Social Services were again called and a permanent placement was found for her.

Rose was a good bit younger than Miss Preston. A happy, plump, middle-aged matron married to a domineering, possessive husband. Dave outwardly was a very pleasant man. It was only as I got to know them better I learnt he dictated what food they ate, decided the clothes she should buy (where he always accompanied her) and even insisted he could cut and perm her hair. Along with all the other things he could control, like friends and family visits. They had four children who adored their mother, but whose lives had been run as Father wished. All had left home by the time I met them. He brought Rose to the surgery. Rose, he said, was tired all the time and no longer coped with getting the evening meal ready for when he came back from work. The aggressive way he said it gave me a hint to his character. He was being inconvenienced. A little questioning revealed she was forgetting things. She would come back with only part of the shopping list he had made for her. Finding words could make her hesitate which he found irritating. Every time I directed a question at her he answered immediately. Eventually I had to be rude and tell him to shut up. Even when she did answer my questions she looked to him for approval first. Rose was quite sure she was making the same meals she always did. When asked what she had cooked yesterday she deferred to Dave. She really had no idea even what day of the week it was.

Dementia sometimes has a physical cause. The commonest is a urinary tract infection. In fact it is frequently the main cause for many an older person. Rose was given blood, urine, blood pressure and all the standard tests, but as expected they were all normal.

During these investigations we had a chance to talk. Dave this, and Dave that. Dave wouldn't like this. Dave wouldn't let her do that. Just faintly I wondered if her condition was a reaction to the submissive life she had led for over thirty years. At that time there was no effective medication to offer, other than sedatives to make both their nights easier. A non-productive visit to the psychiatrist eventually took place after weeks of denial from Dave. Quite rapidly her condition worsened. From having difficulty in dressing she went to not getting dressed. She became increasingly irritable and hard to help. She muttered as she shuffled round and round the house. Then she took to her bed and refused to speak or get up. The children were amazing. They took it in turns to care for her. In all, her illness was only debilitating for about a year before she died at the age of fifty-seven. Her type of dementia is known as pre-senile dementia.

Gemma's dementia took a very different presentation. She forgot appointments. Gemma, a wealthy widow, was vain. Even in her late 70s her weekly hair and nail 'do's were central to her existence. Her hairdresser phoned one day when Gemma's daughter happened to be in the house. She had assumed mother was at her usual appointment. Gemma hadn't turned up for her weekly session. He also pointed out recently her mother was having difficulty in remembering where she had left her car. This made sense to the daughter who had become increasingly concerned about the state of the house and the rotting food in the fridge. Hence the reason she was there to answer the phone when she knew mother would be out. Hastily she finished clearing out the fridge, substituting fresh food for old, and left before she was caught knowing Gemma would have thrown a tantrum if she had known her housekeeping was being questioned.

That evening she came to see me and poured out all her worries. The phone call had precipitated facing up to the obvious problem with Mother. The difficulty here was to get Mother seen medically. She had always refused health checks of any sort. I saw her very occasionally for trivia such as sinus infections and skin rashes but in no way knew her. It is not possible to knock on a door and say 'you need help'. Mother, I was told, had always been short tempered. This had apparently got much worse in recent months even resulting in the daughter being told to get out and never come back. Her driving had become a major cause of concern to all who knew her. Only a series of miracles had avoided serious accidents. Eventually a helpful friend removed the big end of the engine and for some reason no mechanic could be found to repair the car.

Providence again. Gemma developed a lump in her breast. As expected she had ignored it until it had grown to a point where it caused a messy discharge on blouses. She showed the mess to her daughter who then forcibly brought her for consultation. Gemma came almost willingly in the end. A large dollop of authority on my part eventually got her hospitalised and treated with palliative radiotherapy. Too late for anything other than palliative care. A nursing home solved the daughter's problems. At least, as far as the daughter was concerned, for the time being only. Her grandmother and an aunt had had Alzheimer's disease. The daughter was very mindful some things do run in families. Possibly, now well into the twenty-first century, DNA analysis may be able to tell her and even, should she prove to be vulnerable, prevent it with gene therapy.

Dementia is a disease we all dread, both to have it oneself or to have a close member of the family with it. It is so depressing to watch a former competent relative or friend lose their inhibitions and behave differently from their former selves. I have seen some become uncontrollably abusive and use swear words the family had no idea they even knew about. To see a dignified former bank manager 'escape' from his home to run naked down the road in full view of his neighbours is terrible for the family. The chap I remember like this was so aggressive he needed heavy sedation before he could be moved to a place of safety.

There are various medications that delay the disease escalating, but they are only temporary stop-gaps. By the time most present for medical help it is already a bit too late. Thankfully society is far, far kindlier now to those who are demented and supportive of the carers than even twenty years ago. It is caused by shrinkage of the brain itself beyond the normal gradual shrinkage that comes with age. Scans show this clearly. With an ever-aging population there are going to be more and more suffering this disease requiring more and more safe homes and carers.

19. Immigration

No, this is not to discuss the pros and cons of the current situation! During my time in practice we saw refugees from so many countries. Jamaica, Poland, Hungary, Pakistan, Bangladesh and Vietnam just to mention a few.

As a final year medical student in London we had in the vicinity of the maternity hospital where I was studying, a massive influx from Cyprus. At one stage it was said there were more Cypriots in London than in Nicosia! At that time there was no such thing as an ethnic shop. The number one problem was to find food they would eat. England was colder than they were used to, and the food completely alien. Many of the pregnant women were seriously anaemic even before they arrived in this country. The midwives eventually devised the perfect diet the Cypriot ladies would accept and was nutritious. Fish and chips, baked beans and oranges. Plenty of protein in the fish, carbohydrate in the chips, vitamin C in the oranges and above all iron in the baked beans. This, as well as having a pretty balanced diet of vitamins and minerals. The next problem was to keep the Greek Cypriot men from encountering the Turkish Cypriot ones when visiting the wards. Their home living accommodation was desperately crowded with few facilities. Their feuds didn't end because they were now in London. This undoubtedly escalated many of the fights that broke out.

At first my practice was essentially English and Irish. One in four of the households in the immediate vicinity was Roman Catholic. Mostly the men worked on the railways, in the factories or in the numerous shops and warehouses. The women were usually fully occupied with childcare. Also in the 1960s and 70s it was not the norm for wives to go out to work. Within the immediate practice area were rows and rows of two-up, two-down terraced houses. Well into the 1970s many of them did not have bathrooms. Gradually the coal shed and loo were combined and the bathroom entered from the kitchen. Many acquired extensions. The loo was outside, next to the coal shed, in flats made from three- and four-storey Victorian houses. A little further up the hill were semi-detached three- and four-storey houses built close together. In past years these had housed the lower middle classes with the poor little maid in the attic bedroom. Some still had the bedroom bell on the wall by which she could be called at all hours of day and night. Almost all were converted into at least three flats, some four, five or even six units. They proved to be ideal for refugee or housing organisations. Very many of them were bought by them, offering cheap accommodation. At one stage we had so many teenage single mums in these units we were given a second health visitor. Usually they comprised one big bed-sitting room with kitchen facilities in a corner and a shared bathroom and lavatory. Furnishings were minimal – apart from the all-essential TV.

To digress a little – we had an amazing patient who lived in one of these flats who was so distressed to see these hopelessly inexperienced mothers trying to cope with screaming babies she started a daily morning club for them in the church hall close to the surgery. With support from our two health visitors the council was persuaded to pay the rent on the hall. She organised babysitting, pram walking for when the mother needed a break and many other innovations. Many of these young mums were almost, if not completely illiterate. Invariably they insisted on bottle feeding. I was most impressed to find a health visitor with two little bowls and a supply of red tiddly-winks. The jugs were marked to the water level in indelible ink and each time the girl put a level measure of dried milk in the jug she moved a tiddly-wink. Later this wonderfully helpful patient also started the after school key club for children who would have come home to an empty house. At least forty would come every afternoon to be given baked beans on toast or some other food for their tea. The older ones were put in a separate room to do their homework. She deserved a medal. She was also the only person I ever knew who won a major raffle prize. A bright red Mini.

The first immigrants I can clearly remember were the Jamaicans. They became our cheerful postmen, bus drivers and conductors and integrated easily. We saw quite a bit of them in the surgery as they have a very high incidence of raised blood pressure. Then there was a sudden influx of Hungarian and Polish refugees who were re-housed in our practice area following the 1956 uprising. All I came across were gentle, grateful to be in the UK and delightful. One couple that particularly remain in my memory was a former Professor of English and his very sick wife. Her heart failure meant her days were not to be many and my visits frequent. I got to know them well. He was unable to find a similar occupation here to the one he had had in Hungary. His English was good, but not that good. He contented himself with a job sweeping the garage forecourt of the local service station. He expressed his pleasure in being able to support both himself and his wife. I wonder how many UK citizens today would be willing to accept such a situation at all, let alone with pleasure?

We then had an enormous influx from the Indian continent, both from Pakistan and Bangladesh. And a large number of Asians who had fled Africa from Idi Amin. Any sort of appointment system I had tried to organise by then had to be abandoned. Communication was difficult despite most having some command of English. At least the men did. Many women were without any education. New diseases to the UK were becoming common. Suddenly we were dealing with tuberculosis, which had become extremely rare over here. One household had nineteen residents and all were infected bar two small children. Diagnosis of the first one was embarrassing for me. I ordered an x-ray for the wrong reasons. The patient had come with his halting English to complain of a cough, but not a bad one. No story of coughing up blood, loss of weight or anything suspicious. Nothing to hear on listening to his chest either. However, he was anxious,

I was feeling pressurised with work, so rather than spending time explaining my findings I ordered what I thought would be a misuse of the x-ray facilities, but just might put his anxiety to rest. The x-ray showed clear signs of the disease. Next there was the public health essential of getting all the other contacts x-rayed, organising specialist treatment and isolation where necessary. A true marathon. With hindsight I think he must have known he had had previous contact with tuberculosis. As I got to know this extended family it was not usual for him to show anxiety. I shared many conversations with them, followed their progress through Ramadan, learnt a lot about the Muslim faith and their former culture. They were lovely, genuine people who had been through hell in Africa.

For the first time we saw tapeworms – brought in jam-jars – and other worms and nematodes. A lot of malaria, too. We had learnt all about tropical and other overseas diseases at medical school, but they were certainly not at the forefront of a possible diagnosis until this time. It was back to the textbooks. Diagnosis needed a lot more thought. We, as doctors, are reminded that common things are commonest. Tuberculosis, tapeworms, malaria and sickle cell anaemia were not common in the 1960s. Blood tests for sickle cell disease and sickle cell trait needed to be carried out, especially in pregnant women. A nasty, hereditary disorder that can lead to near fatal anaemia. Instead of being round, the red blood cells are distorted and can get stuck in small blood vessels causing strokes and painful episodes. Also they do not last as long as normal-shaped ones, so the patient easily becomes anaemic.

Now people travel so widely, and to the far corners of the earth, it is essential to consider the exotic diseases.

With the Asians came the ethnic shops so there was little problem with their ability to find familiar foods. But their culture differed from ours. Particularly from Pakistan I found the men very protective of their women. As a female doctor my workload increased hugely as the men brought their women to me, not to my male partners, and expected to stay during the consultation, however intimate. Sometimes useful as interpreters, but there were so many occasions I would have wished a few private words with the women. If she came on her own it was usually with a child of school age who could interpret for his or her mother. That could be very difficult too. The age of the young wives often worried me. Always told they were sixteen, it was hard to believe. The husbands were often three times their age. All, of course, arranged marriages. One horrendous episode can never be forgotten. An educated Hindu woman fell deeply in love with a Muslim man she met at university. She came to say goodbye to me explaining they were moving away from London to hide from their families in another big city. They planned to marry, despite vitriolic and threatening objections from both families. I wished her well. About six months later I read in the newspaper she had become the victim of an honour killing.

In the late 1970s we had a couple of dozen Vietnamese boat people moved locally and came to our practice. Language here was almost insurmountable as even their 'health visitor' translator had negligible English. They were voluble, and, a bit like the English, thought the louder they shouted the more easily we would understand. They were somewhat traumatised and needed medical examinations to try and get some sort of basis on which to make a diagnosis. One young woman was found to be diabetic. She was dehydrated, breathing badly and ill, but refused to go to any hospital. She refused to be injected with insulin and became extremely agitated and angry. So did the 'health visitor' who insisted she had been treated with a herbal medicine in Vietnam and had never been ill before. I called one of my partners to come and see if he could find a solution. In the end we prescribed a cocktail of diabetic pills and had to let her go home. I called the London headquarters of the organisation that had homed them to try and find out what this herbal medicine could be. They were unable to help. Inevitably she died. The relatives tried very hard to get me struck off the medical register for refusing to treat her. Fortunately, for me, though not for the patient, the complaint was thrown out. Many times I have tried to find out what the medication in Vietnam could have been. So much simpler than injections and, if it really existed, such a bonus for the thousands who have to inject themselves daily.

Mostly our immigrant population was transient, spreading across the country as they found their feet and integrated, usually with those of the same origin. Almost all enriched our lives.

20. Country Practice

After thirty-five years of a busy multicultural practice my husband and I decided to take early retirement and move to the country. Not too big a culture shock as we were both brought up in the country and only came to suburbia after university. Having latterly been in the habit of seeing my first patient round about 8 a.m. and continuing pretty steadily until at least 6.30 p.m., I decided I was getting older, and would look for part-time work. Three days a week suited me fine in a delightful rural practice. No commuters wanting to be seen as extras at the very beginning or the very end of the day, no staff to look after, no finances to organise, no weekly partners' meetings to discuss progress or otherwise, no Trainee (or Registrar as they are now called) to train and supervise, very few interruptive phone calls – in fact for the first time since starting in General Practice I could spend all my time seeing patients and doing the job for which I had trained. There were still Saturday morning surgeries to be done, but I was happy to be part of the rota.

The biggest shock was the different pace of life. The lovely receptionists were relaxed, knew all the patients and were friends with most of them. I found very quickly the need to be careful about any comment involving a person. During coffee break (yes, there was even time for this) I had a little grumble about our dilatory plumber, only to discover he was related to one of the receptionists. Everyone seemed to be related in some way to anyone one liked to mention. Incomers, like us, existed, but there were not too many of them. Mostly they moved there to be near family. Holiday homes were numerous on the fringes of this practice. They were seen as disruptive, ruling out affordable housing for locals, having poorly kept gardens, empty during the winter and spoiling any sense of community in the villages.

Appointments were at ten-minute intervals with occasional gaps in which to catch up. Sheer luxury! At first I needed the extra time (by newer standards not nearly enough) as I found the locals not too easy to understand. Not so much the dialect, but the meaning they tried to convey. The computer system was well organised and the one familiar to me. For some inexplicable reason when computers were first introduced to practices there were no guidelines on the system to use. As a result several systems evolved, now down to just two. Quite crazy as it is difficult to communicate between them and for a long time a gap between hospital, GP organisations and the system chosen by a particular practice.

One lovely farm labourer caused me to chuckle for days. It should have been sad, but I couldn't help but laugh. He had a bout of nasty bronchitis. He asked me what I was doing tapping away at that machine. I explained I was making a record of his illness and tapping out his prescription of antibiotics for him to collect from the dispensary. He asked what else I had on that there computer. I altered the screen to his home page with address, phone number and relatives recorded. For a long time he stared at the screen. Probably about two whole minutes. He then turned to me with a grin and said: "You can put what you like on that there computer – I can't read." Later I asked in reception if this was common in the area. Yes, it was, and they were always careful with registering patients, particularly those who had left their glasses at home.

My first visit request was nearly a disaster. Because

it sounded urgent and I was duty doctor they put the call straight through to me. The wife's dialect was even stronger than most of the patients I had got to know. I asked for instructions on how to find the farm. "Turn left where they had the straw bales piled up last year, then keep going until you see the sheep in the new fencing etc. etc." I was hopelessly lost and by the time she rang off had even lost her name. Some detective work on the part of the staff found her name and address. One of them thought she knew how to find the track to the farmhouse. Oh, for sat-nav! Or even a mobile phone. I did get there eventually and could deal with the problem.

Another visit really did land me in the muck. This time it was the wife who was ill. Actually it was the farmer himself who rang and it was the wife of one of his labourers who was ill. He said to make sure I had my wellingtons with me. I hadn't, but I did have a sturdy pair of shoes and was sure they would be fit for any walk. I had become a little wiser to country visiting. Not wise enough. They were busy clearing the cattle sheds after the winter and to get to the cottage I had to traverse the gap between sheds and house to reach the cottage itself. I think the farmer was rather amused and thought he had taught me a lesson. Well, I did know, and had been taught in all my training how essential it was to actually listen to the patient. Now I learnt to listen to the caller as well.

My childhood had been largely on a farm and I relished getting back into the jargon, the smells and particularly the animals. Except geese. Geese are better than any burglar alarm and used as such by many farms and smallholdings. My visiting bag took many a bite intended for me. Sometimes one connected – and it hurt. A casual question about the state of the crops or the livestock prompted an immediate response, often half an hour later finding myself enjoying tea and cake to hear the rest of it. Lambing time often found me holding a bottle to feed an orphan lamb.

21. Freedom for Women

This of course only really happened when contraception became reliable. The suffragettes and World War 1 did a great deal for women, but could not control the unplanned and numerous pregnancies that tied women to the home. Marriage or living as a lonely spinster were the only real options open to women.

The 'withdrawal' method has been used since the knowledge of how babies were conceived was known. However, not a reliable method. The odd sperm had a habit of leaking before withdrawal took place. Douches or the insertion of chemicals has been recorded since the sixteenth century. These often had serious consequences such as infection and scarring, and often too with a high failure rate. The sperm had travelled far too quickly to be trapped in the vagina waiting for a douche. In the nineteenth century the cycle of female egg production was discovered, enabling abstinence of intercourse to be taken in the middle of the month – roughly twelve to seventeen days after the first day of her period. For most women this can work. Today there are easy temperature and chemical tests to make this even more a 'safe period'. But, and this is the big but, it needs the co-operation of the male half of the partnership. If he comes home slightly drunk and aggressive no amount of talk about it not being the 'safe period' is likely to add much to marital harmony. Also quite a number of women have either an irregular cycle or a different one from standard. I had a knock on my front door late one evening from a neighbour whose husband had unexpectedly come home on leave from the army. She told me her period was due in about three days' time. At her age of thirty-nine I also thought her fertility would be low anyway. Nine months later she had a beautiful baby boy to add to her grown-up children. We remained good friends!

From 1885 cocoa butter and quinine suppositories were available to insert before intercourse. Their efficacy improved considerably in the 1930s when a spermicide was discovered and used with the cocoa butter. Condoms made from animal intestines were available throughout this time but with much less success than the twenty-first century ones. Vulcanised rubber barrier cones were invented in 1843 to be inserted into the vagina before intercourse. Along with a spermicide this remained the safest method of contraception until 'the pill'. Still used today, they are now made of polyurethane. Female condoms have been available since 1992. They are cumbersome but popular where there is no male co-operation or other method easily available.

Move on to 1957 when 'the pill' became available, free to all. For the first time, providing the woman took it as directed, there was total control over her own fertility. There were very, very occasional exceptions but in those days when the pill was at least seven times stronger than those used today I believe they were patient carelessness. 'The pill' has been revised downwards steadily over half a century to a much medically safer but extremely effective method of contraception. A small percentage taking the pill have experienced blood clots and other even rarer complications. There have been a number of 'pill' scares. Some following serious research, but more blown up from a small-print sentence in a medical journal taken out of context. Remember, men were not happy with the discovery of a truly effective method of allowing women the freedom to leave the home and enter the workplace.

One morning, I believe in the late 1970s, I arrived

to take morning surgery. There was a queue of women halfway down the road waiting to book in with the receptionist, mostly clutching newspapers or bits torn out of one. Unable to get into the reception area I squeezed past the queue, saw a sensible woman I knew well, grabbed her by the arm and took her into the consulting room with me. Rather surprised to be dragged away from the queue she allowed me to read the article. It was a major scare saying women were now going to get breast cancer before they were forty if they were on 'the pill', plus a hugely exaggerated scare on the dangers of blood clots and death. I then sat down and rang our very sensible Medical Officer of Health to ask if he knew anything. Poor man had been researching it for the last hour. His understanding was it was almost pure journalese with miniscule research material. The risk of breast cancer had increased from something like seven in ten thousand to eight. Surely statistically not very significant! The journalist had also unearthed some fatal cases of pulmonary embolism. This may have been partly due to 'the pill' but young people have been dying from this forever. The figure had not been compared with pre-'pill' days. Armed with this information I delivered a mini lecture to the waiting ladies but still offered to discuss it individually if needed.

The intrauterine device may sound even more modern, but the Egyptians knew all about the method 4,000 years ago. They would insert a pebble into the camel's uterus before embarking on a long journey. At the end of the journey they would remove it and the camel could continue her fertility. In the UK it was 1970s before safe ones were available and 1996 before they became even better with hormone release plastics.

There is always a difficulty with the feckless and unreliable lady. Particularly the young. 1974 saw the injectable hormone which could be given every three months allowing a reasonably good period of protection. Much, much better are the implants that have been available from 1993. A simple insertion into the arm gives three years of protection. With the current climate of even younger and more immature girls determined to become sexually active, however well-educated and counselled they may be, this is the method of choice. Huge numbers of parents now come to the surgery with their daughters, often as young as thirteen, asking for them to have the inserted contraceptive. It is a better option than a teenage pregnancy.

Of course it is possible to have one hundred present certainty by a vasectomy for him, or having the tubes tied for her. Both now very widely used.

22. HIV and All That

I did not recognise the disease in the first patient I saw with AIDS. It was 1985 and only just becoming a major topic in the medical publications. It had only just begun to permeate the General Practice journals. He was skeletally thin, obviously very ill with a large strange rash covering his back. Jack had been working in New York for the past two years but as he had become more ill decided to resign his job and move back to the UK. Fortunately (for me only) he knew what was wrong with himself. His partner had died from AIDS six months earlier. He had moved in homosexual circles where more and more of his friends were becoming infected. Despite months of sweating, fever and loss of weight he had been too scared to seek medical help, well aware it would prove expensive and futile. Now, his breathing was becoming increasingly difficult and he was seeking a hospice for his final months. Had he presented a few years later there would have been drugs to prolong his life.

Now there are drugs which can control the infection, but so far there is no cure. The cocktail of drugs is very expensive but enables the victim to live for many years in reasonable health. HIV (Human Immunodeficiency Virus) is a particularly nasty virus thought to have come from primates in central Africa. Researchers re-testing preserved skin and lungs of patients who have died oddly or unexpectedly as far back as 1960 have identified the disease and realise it has been around for a long time. The virus attacks the cells in our bodies that normally fight and protect us from infections, leaving the patient vulnerable to the simplest infection from which he may not survive. It predisposes to certain cancers, particularly Kaopsi's sarcoma, and cervical ones. It spread only by blood and sexual fluids. Drug addicts, those receiving tattoos by uninspected practitioners, babies born to infected mothers and medical staff jabbing themselves with used syringe needles are among those most commonly affected. The wretched virus can live in the body for years without doing any great damage but can then turn into full blown AIDS at any time (Acquired Immune Deficiency Syndrome).

Because so many with HIV are homosexual or

drug addicts there is a stigma attached to the disease. Also an ethical problem. It is going to affect a life insurance plan. Doctors are frequently asked to carry out medicals to ensure the company is not taking any obvious risk. I had one particularly difficult one. I had known Simon and his brother since his birth along with his parents. Simon was extremely clever, getting a first-class honours degree in astrophysics. He was head-hunted for a prestigious job. His parents had come to me in great distress some years earlier (Simon was now twenty-seven) having discovered he was living with a partner in a homosexual relationship. I had also heard via the grapevine who this partner was. They lived in a luxurious flat in Mayfair. It was more than his parents could take. He needed a medical. It specifically asked if there was any risk of HIV infection. They asked if I could help. In some distress I had to state firmly I could not, and would ask them to find someone else to do the medical. They did, but the examiner had to have a report from his GP as to his health to that date. I could honestly say he had had no serious illness to my knowledge. I never knew what happened. Neither he nor his parents came near me again.

An equally, if not more difficult case presented itself to me. John was an international banker with a lovely wife and three children in their early teens. John went to New York on business, drank far too much and got caught up in a group sex situation. Both hetero- and homo-sexual. Next day he was mortified. Instead of going straight home he came in to see me. It appeared he was at serious risk of having contracted HIV. We arranged a blood test. The result, of course, would not be immediate. The dilemma was how to be with his wife. She had had her tubes tied so they did not use any condoms or other protection. Telling her the true story might sound good in advice columns, but in practice would have a lasting, devastating effect on a happy marriage. He could plead tiredness or indisposition for a day or two, but not until the blood test came back. The only other thing I could suggest was to plead extreme weariness the first night, and then have an urgent appointment overseas the next day. He did and spent a few days in Stockholm. With enormous relief the test was clear. How, I wonder, would one have handled it if the result had been positive?

23. Cystic Fibrosis

A very nasty genetic disorder. About one in twenty-five of us carry the gene, so perhaps more surprising there are not more cases.

Thomas arrived a very healthy, lovely-looking lad, weighing in at only two kilos. Instead of a cry there was only a stifled grunt. The midwife had such difficulty sucking out the mucus whilst watching him change to a sickly pallor we sent for a paediatrician and incubator urgently. Both arrived almost immediately. Eventually Thomas began to breathe on his own but we were far from happy. A tentative diagnosis of cystic fibrosis was made.

The severity varies greatly. Life-threatening, disabling and desperately time consuming for the parents. Now, at last, in the twenty-first century, there is real hope of curing such genetic disorders. Since lung transplants have become more successful there is now real hope for the sufferers.

It is caused by a fault in the body's salt and water balance leading to sticky mucus blocking the lungs and interfering with the pancreas, preventing the enzymes needed to digest food from working.

It is often detected at birth when the new-born has particular difficulty with breathing and sticky mucus, like Thomas. More often, as a few months go by, the baby fails to thrive and has a number of chest infections usually needing hospital admissions. Once weaning starts the untreated baby becomes really ill.

Mr and Mrs M. almost lost Thomas after only a few days of life. His rapid admission to a specialist hospital resulted in his survival. Had it been less severe it would nowadays have been picked up by the standard Guthrie test taken by all babies. Thomas needed to be turned upside down several times daily with gentle patting on his back to remove the sticky mucus trying to block his lungs. Not just as a baby, but right through childhood, every day and hanging over the bed when too big to turn upside down. Throughout life. A lengthy process needing skilled physiotherapists to help. Add to this the medicines essential to keeping him alive. Bugs love sticky mucus.

He needed antibiotics, substitute digestive enzymes, among much else. An adult with this disease can take fifty tablets a day, easily.

Thomas was grizzly, slow to feed and very slow to put on weight. He was a great worry to all of us, but fortunate in having devoted and wonderful parents. They were practising Roman Catholics. Eighteen months later Bobby arrived (later they had three unaffected children). He was slightly less severely affected than his brother, but again needed full-time care. Hospital admissions were endless, hospital visits were endless, and organising prescriptions and collecting the vast amount of medication needed was endless. Both boys were unaffected mentally. In fact both were of above average intelligence. At a very young age they accepted their very abnormal diet of virtually pre-digested food. They were co-operative and delightful. At that time, in the 1970s a special diet had been evaluated and was available on prescription. It tasted horrible. But the boys grew and developed slowly, but normally. Because of the time needed for physiotherapy and hospital admissions progress through education was also slow, but, and this gave us all such joy, they both got to university and eventually their degrees. However, Thomas was deteriorating. His lungs were barely functioning and by the age of twenty-nine looked as if he were near his end.

Time had moved on and lung transplants were available. By this time I had left London and was delighted to hear he had had a successful transplant. Bobby, so far, and is, managing a job with computer programming.

It is a hard life. Very restricted diet, massive medication, and physiotherapy several times daily. No sport, a limited lifespan, the latter lengthening year by year as research moves forward. Genetics should sort the problem completely – one day.

24. Difficult Moments

Some were embarrassing, some frightening.

Our next-door neighbour to the Practice, not unreasonably, took exception to the patients parking in front of his house, blocking his exit. He was in the habit of over imbibing and had obviously done a little more than usual to pluck up courage to come in and confront me with it, armed with a broken-off beer bottle. I cannot remember ever being so terrified of anything compared with this. He advanced as I backed towards the window, aiming at my face. I got my hand under the windowsill and pushed the button that I occasionally used to call the next patient. I pushed it repeatedly as he drew nearer. Within inches of my face the door burst open and two receptionists rushed in. He turned and I got out of his way. He fled. It took several cups of tea to recover enough to carry on.

My partner (GP partner!) once had a patient so upset by the refusal to sign a certificate he was hit under the chin and completely knocked out. No, in neither case did we involve the police. With hindsight I cannot think why not.

My husband and I always parked our cars in front of the garage instead of in it. Does anybody use their garage for cars? Gyms, workshops, garden sheds, spare room, office – but not cars. Neither of us was good at locking them. It was the days before integral radios so any radio was vulnerable and often stolen. One morning a couple of police officers arrived when we were having breakfast. They were just a tiny bit aggressive, pointing out ours were the only cars in the road unlocked – and the only cars in the road from which the radios had not been stolen. Eventually we persuaded them we had not stolen any radios and could not explain the reason why ours were untouched.

It was three years before I found the answer. One of my patients came wanting a certificate to say his back was so bad he couldn't attend court. I really could find very little wrong and refused. He got up very angrily and yelled that last time he'd 'done' our road he'd left our cars alone. Never followed that one up, but can guess he'd been 'done' again for something very similar.

One patient, at least he was only my patient for ten minutes, came in and demanded a prescription for a massive dose of female hormone. He'd been over to the USA to have 'the' operation and now needed the medicines to maintain his new female status. Before I could open my mouth he was up on the couch, undressing his lower half to show me how good it was. I closed my mouth and suggested he got dressed again and sat down. Being totally unfamiliar (1980s??) with this condition and unsure whether such prescriptions were allowable on the NHS, I stalled for time to investigate. He flew into a rage, stormed out of the room shouting I was the third lousy, incompetent doctor he had come across. I never saw him again.

One other occasion it was not me that was embarrassed. This young man had been unwise and run into all sorts of venereal problems. Again this was the 1970s and unlikely to be awkward today, but after a long consultation he was about to leave, when he suddenly covered his mouth with his hand and exclaimed, "My God, I've just realised you are a woman!" and fled!

Litigation, or the possibility of it, always was present. Only once did it happen to me and it was incredibly unpleasant despite knowing I had behaved correctly. Butazolidin was frequently used for severe arthritis. It was very effective. Now only given to horses as 'Bute' as far as I know. But it was found to have a rare fatal side effect. It could cause an untreatable blood disorder. Once this was established the drug was banned. This elderly lady was so compromised by her arthritis I had referred her to a Rheumatologist at the local hospital who recommended Butazolidin. She had monthly blood tests. This was obviously not enough because inside a month her blood cells disappeared and she died. Her family went through all the complaints procedures, and eventually, after six months I was called to give my side before the panel. They took precisely ten minutes to clear me, but it was six months of misery waiting for it all to happen.

Afterwards I joined a group of other GPs who would go and sit with colleagues who were under threat of litigation. Some were as guilty as was possible, but others, like myself, were not guilty.

25. The Future

In fifty years the progress of medicine, investigations, diagnosis and treatments has grown astronomically. Sadly, this has its price. It is no longer possible to have a personal relationship with each patient, or to work accurately and assess each case fully, and still get up two or three times during the night. I can remember many a day consulting in a haze and hoping for the best after being up half the night with a difficult delivery or a sick child. Now, with set appointments, a massive increase in possible investigations and an even more massive increase in available treatments, the day is filled to capacity with few, if any breaks from concentrated consultations. There is, too, the spectre of litigation with every patient contact.

I'm also glad to know the hospital juniors no longer work the stupidly long hours we did. For instance, Friday could be a normal day on the gynaecology/obstetric unit. When the rest of the team went home the junior was more or less alone for the weekend with senior help on call. I remember vividly one Monday morning at about 5 a.m. stitching up a mum after a caesarean section and sliding gently to the floor in sheer weariness. I still had to work all the Monday at normal clinics and ward rounds before getting a night's sleep. We learnt tremendously on the job, but it was not best for the patients. Today it has fallen much too far the other way with EU directives preventing junior doctors from getting essential continuity and experience.

When I first went into General Practice we were still measuring drugs in grains, drachms and ounces. Latin was essential. Now it's not at all necessary, and of course, it's all in milligrams, grams and millilitres. Pills were counted out into little boxes, and medicines into bottles. Now almost everything is pre-packed in un-openable strips of twenty-eight or thirty, preventing those on more than one medication from ever matching them up. Some come in child-proof bottles which any three-year-old can open – but we adults cannot. Drugs and medicines – even quite potent ones – were left on the doorstep of the surgery to be collected. There was a baize board in our open porch usually full of prescriptions. An unthinkable practice today! The red tonic and the green tonic were greatly in demand. Also the indigestion and diarrhoea mixtures.

I remember one dear lady who nearly died. "Mixt. kaolin et morph" was frequently prescribed for diarrhoea in adults. The 'morph.' of course being a morphine derivative in liquid form. It could even be obtained without prescription, but as prescriptions were free it rarely was. It needed little imagination to see the occasional person would become addicted to the morphine, despite there being only a little in each bottle. Mary did. She did the rounds of us three partners carefully working out half days and bought another number of bottles 'across the counter'. Record keeping? Forget it. The inevitable happened. Morphine is very constipating. She became so constipated her large bowel blocked! By the time I saw her she needed urgent surgery and very nearly died under the anaesthetic.

Medicine and General Practice have moved on at a colossal pace during the last fifty years. I keep saying this, but it needs repeating. Hundreds and hundreds of times more discoveries than in the last four thousand years. People and patients have remained much the same. The problems presented now are perhaps a little different, but not greatly so. Effective medicines have largely evolved during my fifty years, though penicillin and sulphonamides are just a little older. Until then there was remarkably little change in consultations and medicines from Ancient Greek times. The Egyptians were far more knowledgeable than the British right up to the seventeenth century, if not the eighteenth. A bit of a major advance in late Victorian times with the discovery of antiseptics and anaesthesia.

When I started as a doctor it was at the very beginning of a trial of a drug that actually reduced high blood pressure. Prior to the early 1960s deaths from the effects of high blood pressure in young people were not uncommon. Now there are a huge number of highly effective medicines and no one should be other than fully treated. Duodenal or stomach ulcer patients were commonly kept in hospital on milk diets for a month or more and frequently came to operation. Medical wards were full of such patients. Surgery for ulcers is now a rare emergency. Almost all are easily treated by medication in General Practice. Having an appendix out was at least a week in hospital – now probably not even an overnight stay. Keyhole surgery has arrived. Replacement hips, knees, shoulders etc. are even more recent successful operations. Even thirty years ago they were uncommon and not always such good results as has become the norm today.

As for post heart attack or angina surgery, this is now more common than an appendectomy. It evolves with more and more lives saved every day. Instead of needing the ribcage opened and enduring a painful recovery period most are dealt with by inserting flexible tubes into arteries via a plastic tube inserted into an artery. These often carry little stents (tubes) to be left in the heart arteries allowing the blood to flow freely again. In the pipe-line are even newer drugs programmed to get rid of the cholesterol plaques that block the arteries. A heart attack used to mean at least a week or two in hospital, followed by several weeks' convalescence and an uncertain future. Now in a couple of days with a stent or two the patient is all but back to normal. Prevention and early detection of heart disease has progressed enormously. Simple blood tests now reveal the high-cholesterol patients, those with raised blood sugars along with other relevant tests. Taking the blood pressure is routine for all patients. Even slightly high pressures are treated energetically. As research discovers how important the levels are in increasing longevity the ideal readings seem to become even lower.

I'm not going through every disease in the book, but there is a steady progression of research and such enormous advances in treatments available that General Practice becomes increasingly busy with a constant need to update. Effective treatments are escalating, including treatments for cancer and abnormal genetics. Gone, I fear, is the old-fashioned traditional family doctor who followed you and your family from birth to grave. He or she is replaced by one who in this computerised age has full access to your medical history and can offer real, up-to-date and holistic treatment.

Printed in Great
Britain
by Amazon